THE ROMANS AT RIBCHESTER

The Romans at Ribchester

Discovery and Excavation

B. J. N. Edwards

Centre for North-West Regional Studies
University of Lancaster
2000
Title Editor: David Shotter
Series Editor: Jean Turnbull

The Romans at Ribchester

This volume is the 40th in a series published by the Centre for North-West Regional Studies at the University of Lancaster. A list of the other titles which are available is at the back of the book.

Published by the Centre for North-West Regional Studies, University of Lancaster

Designed and typeset by Carnegie Publishing Ltd,
Carnegie House, Chatsworth Road, Lancaster LA1 4SL

Printed and bound in the UK by The Cromwell Press, Trowbridge, Wilts

British Library Cataloguing-in-Publication Data
A CIP catalogue record for this book is available from the British Library
ISBN 1-86220-085-8

Contents

List of Illustrations

Foreword

Ribchester's Roman fort and settlement have consistently excited the interest of antiquarians, historians and archaeologists, as well as of the general public. Many factors have contributed to this – the drama of a fort that has been partly eroded by a river, the richness and importance of individual finds that have been made over the years, the fact that the site has a 'dedicated' museum with a history of its own, the significance of the historical questions that have been posed about Roman Ribchester; last, but not least, there is the sheer attractiveness of the village and its setting. A book, which is devoted largely to the history of discovery and of changing interpretations of Roman Ribchester, is appropriate too, providing, as it does, a compelling companion to excavation – reports already published and still to come.

Ben Edwards has the distinction of having been the first County Archaeologist in the country – a recognition of him as well as a tribute to the foresightedness of the Lancashire County Council in the early 1960s; it was a post which he held until his retirement in 1995. Although Ribchester is one of a number of Roman sites in the county which were his professional concern, it is also one that has excited his particular interest; this has manifested itself in his membership of the bodies concerned with the upkeep and development of the museum, and in his involvement over the years in the publication of finds and excavation-reports.

This is a book which will inform and give pleasure: it will also be a valuable addition to the bibliography of an important and often tantalising Roman site.

David Shotter
(February, 2000)

Preface

This book owes a great deal to a great many people. First of these is A. F. Hall, teacher of history, who first put a trowel in my hands and engendered an enthusiasm which endures to this day. Second is Eric Birley, whose decision to admit me to the college of which he was Master introduced me to my university and also to a wider archaeological world whose representatives passed through the Archaeology Department, then in its wooden hut in the grounds of the college. In that college I met Michael Jarrett, near contemporary and friend, who enabled me to become part of that world. And, finally, in this context, comes John Wallis, Rector of Ribchester, who invited me to join the Museum Committee and thus started 35 years of my association with the Roman fort there. All of these have now left us, and I like to think they look down with indulgence on my puny efforts to emulate them. To name all the other people whose help has enabled me to learn about Ribchester would over-tax alike the available space and my memory. Suffice it to say that my awareness of debt to successive Museum Curators, Chairmen and members of the Museum Committee and other colleagues and friends is not therefore less. Among these I must name particularly my collaborator in other writings on Ribchester, Peter Webster. Some of them may find their ideas somewhat curiously represented, and I must crave their forgiveness and acknowledge that what appears in the following pages is 'a poor … ill-favour'd thing, but mine own'. One more point must be made in this catalogue of indebtedness: however much material and however many ideas have been passed on to me by the multitude of people mentioned or referred to above, none of them would have got to the stage of being printed without the help of my wife, Margaret. Her guidance in matters of language, her gift of listening and contributing to mind-clearing discussion and her gentle but effective nudging were all essential parts of the writing of this book. All I can do in return is to thank her and offer her the result in the hope that she enjoys it.

Acknowledgements

In addition to the acknowledgements of the Foreword, I must particularly thank those who gave permission for the reproduction of illustrations (named in the captions); the Lancaster University Archaeological Unit, who allowed me to have a pre-publication copy of the report on the excavations in the churchyard extension, of which I have made relatively little use because the primacy of publication in such matters must go to those involved; and Dr D. C. A. Shotter, F.S.A., who read the text to its improvement, but who bears no responsibility for its contents.

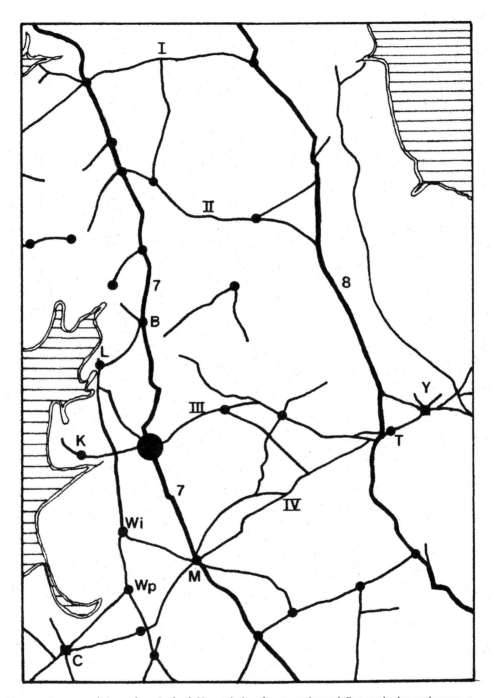

Figure 1. Roman roads in northern England. Uncertainties of route are ignored. Forts and other settlements at or near road junctions are indicated. Hadrian's Wall and its associated works are omitted. Indicated by numbers or letters are: I – IV, the four cross-Pennine routes referred to; the two legionary fortresses, C – Chester and Y – York; the Margary numbers of the two north-south roads, 7 and 8. Also forts etc. at B – Burrow in Lonsdale, L – Lancaster, K – Kirkham, Wi – Wigan, Wp – Wilderspool, M- Manchester and T – Tadcaster.

CHAPTER ONE

The setting of the fort, the Roman road system and the Roman name

The sites of Roman forts were obviously selected with great care and skill. They can be viewed as the result of a threefold assessment, of which two elements were military and the third not specifically so. First there is the general setting. Given that the siting of forts is closely linked with the layout of roads, as is generally accepted, it would be obvious that a fort would be necessary in the vicinity of the junction between a route running north-south to the west of the Pennines and a cross-Pennine route. The possibilities for routes of the latter type are fairly restricted. If one accepts the Roman roads numbered by Margary 7 and 8 (Margary 1978) as being those forming the main north-south routes from the legionary fortresses of Chester and York respectively to the northern frontier, wherever that might lie at any given time, there are really only four Roman crossings of the Pennines joining those main roads: the Tyne gap, occupied first by the Stanegate and later by Hadrian's Wall; the Stainmore route, from Scotch Corner to Penrith, or *Cataractonium* to *Brocavum* in Roman terms; the route from the vicinity of Tadcaster (*Calcarium*) up the valley of the Wharfe to the area of Skipton and then down the Ribble valley to Ribchester and beyond; and, finally, the direct route between the two legionary fortresses, which leaves York for Tadcaster, crosses the hills north-east of Manchester and passes *via* that fort to Chester. The first and third of these routes never attain 800 feet above sea level. The importance of Ribchester at the end of the 'mountain stage' of the third of them is evident.

The second part of the assessment of where to build a fort must have been the consideration of immediate military factors like vulnerability to attack. Here, the site of Ribchester, like that of many Roman forts, demonstrates the difference between pre-Roman, Roman and post-Roman thinking. Beside a river at the bottom of a broad, open valley would have been acceptable as a military site neither before nor after the Roman period. However, Roman arms, both in the technical sense of 'tools of the trade' and in the wider sense of trained manpower, were superior to those of the barbarians. If it is true that Hadrian's Wall was not designed as a structure *on* which to sit and wait for attack, an auxiliary fort was certainly not a structure *in* which to sit and wait; but Roman defence seems to have been based on attack, and so long as the fort site was not such that unobserved intruders could reach it easily, it did not need to be on a near-inaccessible hilltop. Nor, of course, did it need to take account of the possibility of attack with some form of artillery. Only Roman forces had such equipment in the first four centuries AD.

The third set of criteria to be met by a Roman fort site were those relating to the establishment of any form of settlement. Some of these were general, such as the necessity for an adequate water-supply. Some were more particular to the requirements of the Roman army, including especially a reliable food supply for men and beasts. While this might seem to be a general requirement for any form of settlement, response to it was vastly modified by the situation of the

Roman army. While food was necessary, the garrison did not have to produce it (we are speaking of the first century, when the fort was first sited and occupied). The logistical organisation of the Roman army, using the road system to which reference has already been made, would ensure that supplies reached the fort as necessary.

Having made the threefold assessment, we can make some general observations. We know comparatively little about how the Roman army got its food supplies. Exaction in various ways from the native population is presumably the answer, and it would obviously be desirable that supplies should travel the minimum distance. But at least the fort did not have to be sited in country which could support its inhabitants. Insurance against any difficulties in supply was also present in the form of the fort granaries, which could store enough food for a long period.

The situation of the fort, similarly, did not have to take account of the source of other supplies. Long-distance well-organised trade in bulky commodities is readily demonstrable in the case of pottery, and therefore possible in that of other materials. For example, among agricultural products, the Roman army used much leather, and this could have been transported long distances if necessary. Indeed, there is a case to be made for the suggestion that the roads which linked Roman forts were at least as important for the supply of those forts as they were for any military action based on them.

The relationship of the siting of Roman forts to the layout of roads is an interesting one. Clearly, although related, they were to some extent independent of one another. Whichever decision came first, the siting of many Roman forts, including Ribchester, just *off* the line of the nearby road, demonstrates this. Roads were clearly built with long-distance, and perhaps very long-distance, objectives. That is to say that a road would aim perhaps twenty miles ahead, perhaps two hundred.

One can imagine a scenario in which the Roman High Command would decide on the route of one road or more, and decide therefore that forts were needed at certain points along those roads. Perhaps less likely (or less commonly, for it is not necessary that either system should have been the only one) it is possible to think of a general deciding that a fort was necessary at a particular site, and that the roads would have to be built to service it.

Whatever the reality of such imaginary events, taking place, perhaps, in a legate's tent, Ribchester demonstrates very well that on the ground there was a degree of independence between the siting of roads and that of forts. (For further consideration of the roads, see Edwards 1998a).

The south-north road in the vicinity of Ribchester (Margary 7b) comes over the hills from Manchester. There are problems about the precise route of that road. It travels on what is basically one alignment all the way, but it has a curious 'side-step' about half-way, in the area of Affetside. There is also a rather longer distance than usual between the forts of Manchester and Ribchester. Nevertheless, the general route is not in doubt, and the alignment continues on the north side of the Ribble. This probably means that the crossing point, which has been destroyed by the downstream migration of the Ribble's meanders in post-Roman times, lay on that alignment. Dog-legs and zig-zags in Roman roads in order to reduce the gradients when approaching and leaving river crossings are known, but do not seem likely to have been necessary, given the fairly gentle incline of the Ribble valley side in that area. The alignment, however, passes some 750 yards (680 metres) to the east of the fort.

The site of the fort was probably chosen for more local reasons, which can be demonstrated using map evidence. One has to bear in mind that the destruction of part of the fort by the river shows us that the river has moved its course considerably since Roman times. Indeed, it is a very important example which shows in action, clearly and with a time-scale, a process which is easy to describe but less easy to demonstrate.

Wherever exactly the river lay in Roman times, it is clear that today, after it has passed Sale Wheel, some 3000 yards (2720 metres) upstream from Ribchester, it begins to meander downstream of the site of Ribchester Bridge. Indeed, that bridge is not in Ribchester at all, and owes its siting to the presence of firm rock for its foundations. The meanders are only just beginning where Ribchester lies, and there are then five of them between there and Preston. In that stretch of river, few roads reach the river bank and there is no bridge; but throughout that stretch the high meander bluffs preclude the

siting of a Roman fort. Such a fort would have had to be either on a meander bluff, with no easy way down to the river, or on a frequently-flooded area immediately opposite such a bluff, again with no route up its face. Those meander bluffs, by chance, are neatly defined by the 100 foot contour, and it is just downstream of Ribchester that that contour reaches the edge of the meander belt, which it then follows all the way downstream to Preston. Put another way, the site of Ribchester is the last place, as one travels downstream, where a gentle slope down to both river banks could be found.

While the precise course of the river in Roman times has not been ascertained, the meander which has eroded part of the site must then have lain upstream. This might

Figure 2. Aerial view of Ribchester. In the foreground is Lower Alston Farm; between it and the church is Anchorholme; to the right of the church the Parish Hall with its axis more or less east-west and the Museum 1914 building at right angles to it; nearer the river is Churchgates, while the large building surrounded by trees is the Rectory. (Photographer unknown)

well have meant that to reach the north-south road by going straight out of the north-east gate (the *porta praetoria* of the stone fort) would have necessitated a crossing of the river. It is therefore much more likely that any such road led in a much more northerly direction to the main north road, or led only into the *vicus*, possibly to some prominent semi-official building such as the bath-house or a temple.

Similarly, there is evidence that the north-west gate (*porta principalis sinistra* of the stone fort) may have opened onto both a road towards Lancaster and a westward road towards the fort at Kirkham. This would have left the gates to the south-west (*porta decumana*) and south-east (*porta principalis dextra*) with purely local functions. Indeed, such a situation must always have been the case with any 'standard' Roman fort not situated exactly on the crossing of two long-distance roads which could enter by its four main gates.

Let us then examine the courses of the roads which radiate from Ribchester. Though Leland made no mention of them, Camden knew them. 'And the port high waies come directly hither, raised up with eminent causeis: one from Yorke, another out of the North, through *Bowland-Forrest*, a spacious peece of ground, which as yet is most evidently to be seene for many miles together'. This is echoed by Stukeley, writing in 1725, who said, 'There is a lane goes down, north of the city … At the end of this lane is the street which is a Roman road, running directly northward up the fell, called Green-gate: it passes over Langridge [*sic*], a great mountain named from it, so through Bowland forest: it appears green to the eye'.

Though Camden mentioned the York road, it is the north road (Margary 7c) which has attracted most attention. Indeed, it is a fascinating road. As already mentioned, the alignment up Longridge Fell (which rises only a little over a thousand feet from Ribchester, despite Stukeley's designation of 'mountain')

is that which the road has been following south of the Ribble. The prospect where the road tops Longridge Fell (below 950 feet – not the highest point of the Fell) is a splendid one. In front lies the valley in which the Hodder flows west, south, then east, to pass round the eastern end of the Fell and join the westward flow of the Ribble behind the observer. Flowing eastward in front is the little river Loud, which joins the Hodder shortly before it turns south. Usually almost invisible, this river sometimes appears as a broad brown ribbon of flood water. The whole of the valley is dotted with clumps of trees and houses, and centred on the village of Chipping. The Roman observer would, of course, have seen none of these. It would be fascinating to know just what evidence of human activity he *could* see.

Whatever the answer to that question, there are natural phenomena which both modern and Roman observer could make out, if the weather were clear. North and west the sea can be discerned. North-west there is a whaleback hill which derives its modern name from a later use – Beacon Fell. Then, directly in front, is a wall of hills which forms the southern flank of the Bowland massif. Parlick Pike, Fairsnape, Wolf Fell, Ward's End and Burnslack are ranged in front. Clearly there was no way for the road to penetrate northwards there. The reasons behind the decision to turn eastward and then northward again are interesting, but beyond our scope here. The manner of the eastward turn is still evident, however. The modern road does it too for a short distance, and good visibility will show the present-day traveller, as it did the Roman, that he is heading directly for the summit of Pen-y-Ghent. Down in the valley, beyond the Hodder, which was the Yorkshire boundary until 1974, another section of modern road follows the Roman, and, tree-lined, stands out, making a sight-line for the great hill on the horizon.

After this dramatic view, the courses of the other Roman roads from Ribchester may seem tame. Eastwards, the York road (Margary 72) proceeds up the Ribble valley, passing north-west of Whalley and south-east of Clitheroe. It begins to diverge from the Ribble valley in the vicinity of Chatburn, and passes over into Airedale west of Skipton. Near Clitheroe, several parish boundaries follow its line, and today it is partly lost beneath the Whalley-Clitheroe by-pass. Excavation at one point on the line prior to the construction of the by-pass showed that the road was a hollow way worn in the limestone, suggesting that prolonged post-Roman use had removed the constructed surface it would undoubtedly have had in Roman times. It is frequently assumed, tacitly or otherwise, that many Roman roads continued in use into later times. This is an intriguing little piece of actual evidence to lend support to that idea.

There is a little uncertainty as to the line of this road close to Ribchester. If we follow it back from Chatburn, it runs nearly south-west for about six miles. Then, just after having crossed the Calder near Whalley, it swings a few degrees north, in the neighbourhood of Hacking Hall, Billington. This line brings it to the modern road by Marles Wood, at the top of the slope of the Ribble's banks down to Salesbury Hall. Here is a recently-constructed car park (1991–92), and traces of the road were seen when it was made. The same line, if projected, would cut the line of the north road at right angles exactly on the river bank, which sounds very attractive. But we must remember that the river will not have been precisely there in Roman times, and in any case this line cuts into the much-dissected river bank slope, which may have been further forward in Roman times but cannot have been further back. The Ordnance Survey swings the line a few degrees north again at Salesbury Hall and brings it to the river bank near Ribchester Bridge, but there does not seem to be any observed evidence for this precise line.

Having looked north and east, if we continue our clockwise sweep we come to the road south, to Manchester (Margary 7b). As we have observed, this runs on the same alignment south of the Ribble as the section on the southern slope of Longridge Fell. This makes good sense, as the next point southwards at which the alignment changes is Rushton's Height in Darwen, which, at over 1000 feet above sea level, is the highest point the road reaches between Ribchester and Manchester. The change here is less than 10° further east of south, but this enables the road to avoid some of the worst country in Turton, which it would have had to negotiate if the direct line between Jeffrey Hill and Manchester had been adopted. The total distance, Jeffrey Hill to Manchester (about 37 modern miles or 40 Roman miles), is scarcely affected by the deviation from straight.

If the southward road from the fort is fairly simple both to discern and to describe, that to the westward (Margary 703) is neither. It is best considered by following its approach to Ribchester from the west. A line, known as the Danes' Pad – (Pad is connected with the word 'path'; the attributon to the Danes may be just a fanciful attribution of an ancient structure to vaguely known people of the past, or Norsemen may in fact have used it) – was recorded in the nineteenth century running east from Kirkham (where Roman presence was early recognised). It also ran westward from Kirkham, and its destination in that direction has produced much sterile debate. East of Kirkham, however, it seemed likely to be a road to Ribchester. It differed from most Roman roads in being a gentle curve for most of its line. In the northern outskirts of Preston the presence of Watling Street Road supported the attribution, and the road was seen east of Preston on the north bank of the Ribble.

Somewhere in the parish of Alston, however, the clues dried up, and it is very difficult to find a suitable line because of the presence of a number of deeply-incised right-bank tributaries of the Ribble. The obvious way for the Romans to have avoided the difficulties created by these would have been to cross them as high as possible in their courses, and here it may just be worth noting that both Lightfoot Lane, to the north of Preston, and the main road through the village of Grimsargh, to the east, are on a direct line between Kirkham and Ribchester. Other evidence is lacking, however, and one has to remind oneself that not only was the line of the road east of Red Scar known early enough to give its name to Roman Road Farm, but also the road was excavated in advance of the construction of Roman Road Industrial Estate in the 1970s. Evidence of it was also seen during the construction of an astronomical telescope at Alston Hall in 1978.

It has to be said that Margary's comment in connection with the line of this road west of Ribchester is less than satisfactory. He says, 'but the alignment [from Ribchester] to Fulwood now seems to be obstructed by the wide loops of the river Ribble, though no doubt this active river has changed its course in detail quite considerably since Roman times'. This is true as far as it goes, but it ignores the fact that the meander belt, defined as we have seen by the 100-foot contour, must have been in existence below Ribchester in Roman times, and there is no suggestion that the river ran outside that narrowly defined belt at any stage in post-Glacial times.

Whatever expedient was in fact adopted to deal with the difficult country between Alston Hall and Ribchester, the road seems to have entered the fort by approaching the northwest gate at a very oblique angle and turning fairly abruptly into it. The evidence was observed in the 1990–91 churchyard extension excavation.

From that same gate issued yet another road. This (Margary 704) ran northwestwards on or near the line of the modern road from Ribchester to Longridge. Where that road turns to the west near the Cross Keys Inn, the Roman road ran on past Written Stone Farm and up the side of Longridge Fell. Whether it did so as marked on the O.S. map, in a straight line, or, as Margary suggests, at an oblique angle to the slope to reduce the gradient, is unknown. The line of the descent of the Fell on its north face is similarly disputable, as is the course of the road from there on. It is presumed to be aiming at the south east end of a straight section of road running south eastwards from Galgate. At this point the modern road crosses the Wyre on a bridge dated 1762 and known as Street Bridge from the name of the nearby farm. Between the foot of the north face of Longridge Fell and this point there are steeply incised valleys (Brock, Calder, Grizedale Brook), the whaleback of Beacon Fell and the spur of the Forest of Bowland where the modern road crosses the saddle of Harris End Fell. The course of a possible Roman road through all this is very difficult to determine.

Despite the uncertainties in detail, particularly north and west of the fort, the fort's nodal position in the Roman road layout must be clear. What is not possible to demonstrate, however, is the dating of these roads. It seems reasonable to suggest that the north-south road (Margary 7) must date from shortly after the conquest of the area, though probably slightly later than the 'estuaries' road (Margary 70). The cross-Pennine link is unlikely to be much later. Other roads, such as the possible link to Lancaster *via* Street and the westward road to Kirkham, are more problematical. Out on its limb in the Fylde, the fort at Kirkham may have required, or been thought to require at first, only a link to the 'estuaries' road (Margary 70) joining Wilderspool (near Warrington), Walton-le-Dale (south of Preston) and Lancaster *via* the lowest crossing points of the Mersey, Ribble and Lune respectively.

As far as the Roman name of the Ribchester fort is concerned, we are lucky in that there is effectively no doubt of this. The best way of being sure of the Roman name of a site is to have an inscription which gives the name or a version of it; and in the case of Ribchester we have exactly that, in an adjectival form.

This is recorded on the Apollo statue base (RIB 583)* which is, of course, one of the earliest recorded inscriptions from the site. This refers to the army unit for whose welfare the monument was dedicated as N(UMERI) EQ(UITUM) SARM(ATARUM) BREME-TENN(ACENSIUM) – the unit of Sarmatian horsemen of Bremetennacum. This is taken to indicate that the correct nominative form is Bremetennacum, though Rivet and Smith (1979, 277) say fiercely that the doubling of the 'N' has no authority. Nevertheless, this is by far the most frequently used form today, occurring, for example, on the Ordnance Survey Map of Roman Britain and in the title of Richmond's (1945) paper, and is now supported by the form used in one of the writing tablets found at *Vindolanda*.

This inscription enables us to identify other, more corrupt, forms in three surviving documents. These are: (1) The Antonine Itinerary (AI), a second century road-book or list of places along roads; (2) The Ravenna Cosmography (Rav.), a geographical document compiled *c.* A.D. 700 in Ravenna and consisting of a list of places in various geographical areas; its information for Britain can be shown to relate to Britain in Imperial times (i.e. prior to A.D. 400); and (3) The Notitia Dignitatum (ND), a late Roman military list.

There is no need here to go any further into the extremely voluminous literature about the antecedents and date of all three of these. We need only note that they give the name of Ribchester thus – AI – BREMETON-NACI or BREMETONACI; Rav. – BRESNETENACI VETERANORUM; ND – BREMETENRACO, BREMETEMRACO, BREMETERACO.

In case it is thought that the differences between the forms of the name, both between these three sources and within them, imply some differences in the actual name of the

* RIB throughout = Collingwood and Wright 1965.

fort, it should be emphasised that we do not have original documents surviving from the Roman period, or even from the eighth century. All our documents survive only in medieval copies, and these, like all documents written prior to the invention of printing, could be reproduced only by manual copying. All copyists are liable to errors caused by such things as carelessness or failure to understand the original from which they are copying. Copyists who were employed to copy documents, with no other interest than finishing in order to be paid, might be thought to be particularly prone to error, and of course, the exact form of a name not known to the copyist could not be checked by the context, as an ordinary piece of text might.

If these various considerations are accepted, there is no doubt of the general form of the Roman name for Ribchester. But at one time there was indeed a real doubt and a great deal of research and effort went into attempts to be sure. The doubt arose because, although it is easy enough to take the various forms of the name beginning 'Bremet -' and discuss what was its true form, we must also be sure that this name was really that of Ribchester and not of some other Roman site. The inscriptional evidence makes this certain today, but the relevant inscription, weathered and damaged as it is, was not read with certainty until fairly recently. Prior to that time, the chief method of identifying a Roman name with the correct site was to take a list of names such as that in the Antonine Itinerary. Assuming first, that you could pin down one or two of them with reasonable certainty; second, that all the sites on a given route were known and were included in the list; and third, that the direction of travel of the list was known; then, and only then, would it be possible to assign names to a whole series of sites.

Unfortunately, attempts were made in the past to do this; but not all the conditions above were certainly fulfilled. This meant that the same list of names, read in opposite directions and including or excluding certain sites, could give any one site, such as Ribchester, a variety of names. Tables of attempts of this sort can be found in Watkin (1883, 36) and elsewhere. They are of historic interest only, but must be mentioned because they account for the fact that different names have been assigned to the site in the past.

Further complications were added by attempts to show that one or other of the sites named in Ptolemy's *Geography* was Ribchester. Ptolemy was a second century Roman who lived at Alexandria, where the normal language was Greek rather than Latin. His *Geography* consists of lists of geographical locations (some towns, some natural features such as estuaries, promontories and so forth). All of these were assigned co-ordinates of latitude and longitude which could be plotted. Ptolemy could acquire the information for such a compilation only from the evidence of travellers or those who had served in Britain, the quality of which varied. Difficulties also arise from the method of transcribing numerals in Greek, which involves the use of letters of the alphabet with additional marks like accents or apostrophes. These, of course, were even more susceptible to copyists' errors than names, referred to earlier.

Plotting Ptolemy's coastal co-ordinates gives an outline of the British Isles which is recognisable but distorted. It is therefore very difficult to be sure what place is meant by a spot plotted inland, unless the name is already known or suspected from other sources. Further, since the information came from many sources, it is not possible to use the relative position of any two sites to identify either of them.

In the case of Ribchester, *Rigodunum* from Ptolemy was often put forward, but this was no more than guesswork, and etymological considerations make it more likely that this was a hillfort, possibly Ingleborough. Equally, in the case of the Antonine Itinerary, the next site after Manchester, which was always accepted to have been called something like *Mancunium* (*Mamucium* is now thought to be more accurate) was *Coccium*. There being no known Roman site on the direct route between Manchester and Ribchester, difficulties with the distances involved were dealt with by juggling with possible copying errors. *Coccium* is increasingly applied today to the site at Wigan, the road route being assumed to have taken a dog-leg, but there is no evidence to support the attribution of the name.

It may be thought that errors made in the past in the assignment of a Roman name to Ribchester were rendered irrelevant by the certainty of its actual name. In one way this is true, but in any perusal of the earlier literature of the site the reader will find himself reading about *Coccium, Rigodunum* and other names which will be merely puzzling if their sources are not understood.

CHAPTER TWO

The Early Investigators

Most people are fascinated by traces of man's past, but in order to investigate archaeological evidence it is necessary, first, to be able to recognise it, and, second, to have the curiosity to carry the study further than that. To-day, we can only know of someone's investigations if they leave some record of them. This generally means a written record, though occasionally the record is preserved and transmitted by word of mouth. It is as a result of one such verbal transmission that we know that someone in the past was at least capable of recognising some of the traces of earlier human activity at Ribchester, though it is unlikely that the investigation was carried any further.

The evidence for this recognition lies, of course, in the name of the village. The -chester termination, as we now have it, is the result of the naming of the place in one or more of the dialects of Old English, the tongue of the Anglo-Saxons, with a name which included a version of the Old English ceaster, deriving ultimately from the Latin castra. This word ceaster means that the people who gave the village its name saw remains of a fairly substantial structure, and in most such cases that means a Roman structure, as at Ribchester. Literate Anglo-Saxons would have known that the island of Britain had been invaded by the Romans – Bede and other writers, some of whose works have not come down to us, would have told them so – but literate Anglo-Saxons were probably few and far between, especially in the north of England, and it is more probable that the name merely recognised the presence of fortifications from an unspecified former age.

Certainly if any Anglo-Saxon did more than notice the remains, we have no record of it. But those who did notice it, and used the name, spoke more than one dialect of Old English. Our earliest record of the name (See Ekwall 1922) is that given in the *Domesday Book* of 1086, which is *Ribelcastre*, although *Ribbecestre* is found as early as 1202, and similar forms are used throughout the thirteenth century. In the fourteenth century forms with the -*aster* or -*astre* ending are common, usually with the *ch*- of the present form preceding it. So we have *Ribelcastre* in the late eleventh century, *Ribbecestre* and similar forms in the thirteenth, and *Ribelchaster* and similar forms in the fourteenth. Just why Ribchester settled in its present form while Lancaster acquired the -*caster* ending is not known, but it has been observed that most -*caster* names occur in areas of Norse influence. For what it is worth, there seem to be no -*chester* forms recorded for Lancaster.

The first part of the name is, of course, derived from that of the river by which the village stands, and it is sad that we do not have a convincing derivation for the name Ribble. It is probably British – that is, Celtic as opposed to Anglo-Saxon (Germanic) – in origin, but that is all we can say.

Whenever it was that the Anglo-Saxon people began to call the village 'the old fort on the Ribble', many hundreds of years passed before anyone looked at the Roman remains, recognised them as ancient, and made a record of the fact. The man who did so was a remarkable one. He is known to us as John Leland, for thus he spelt his name; but it is at least possible that his family originated only a few miles from Ribchester, and that we should recognise this more readily had he used the spelling Leyland more often. By the time of his birth, about 1506, some of the family were possibly living further south in Lancashire, in the neighbourhood of Leigh. His immediate family were probably more influential than wealthy, for John went to St Paul's School in London, his expenses paid by one Thomas Myles. That his benefactor's money was well spent is shown by the fact that John proceeded to Christ's College, Cambridge, where he took his B.A. in 1522. He went on to study at All Souls', Oxford, and in Paris, and returned to England a very well educated young man.

In 1525, after taking Holy Orders, he was tutor to the younger son of the Duke of Norfolk, and by 1530 had become the King's Library Keeper and a royal chaplain. He held four church benefices in plurality, and was thus well provided for. By 1533, he was the King's antiquary – a unique appointment – and had the royal commission to search for English antiquities in monastic libraries and all other places 'where secrets of antiquity were deposited'.

Leland saw the despoliation of the monastic libraries at the Dissolution, and petitioned Thomas Cromwell, unsuccessfully, to extend his commission to enable him to collect the manuscripts for the King's Library. Between at least 1536 and 1542 he travelled the length and breadth of the kingdom, recording in the notes of his 'itineraries' everything he could learn of antiquities. His notes were intended to be the basis of a great work on the History and Antiquities of the Nation, but were not published in his lifetime. Sadly, as the *Dictionary of National Biography* expressed it, 'his antiquarian studies overtaxed his brain and he became incurably insane'. He died in 1552, and was buried in a London church which was destroyed in the Great Fire and not rebuilt.

It is such a commonplace of English topographical writing to start with Leland's description that it is worth recalling how much of a pioneer he was, and such strictures as that in the *DNB*, which says that the *Itinerary* 'reads like a mass of undigested notes', do him less than justice, for that is exactly what they were.

Of Ribchester he notes '[It] ... is now a poore thing. It hath beene an auncient towne. Great squarid stones, voultes, and antique coynes be founde ther: and ther is a place wher that the people fable that the Jues had a temple'. It will be observed that he makes no mention of the Romans, but his record of the local legend of a Jewish temple is interesting. Christians were felt, in medieval times, to be barred from usury (meaning money-lending in any form, not the exaction of exorbitant interest) by biblical proscription. Jews were under no such ban. As a result, they became the financiers of Europe, and thus among its wealthiest inhabitants. In the manner of wealthy men, they were the most up-to-date, and frequently had the first stone houses at a time when most dwellings used much timber. As a consequence, some of their houses have survived, as in Lincoln and Bury St Edmunds; but in addition the ruins of obviously substantial structures whose builders were unknown were ascribed to them – hence, probably, the Ribchester legend which Leland recorded.

Leland made one other observation which was to have longer-lasting results than his other remarks. By noting 'It flouith and ebbith in Ribyl most communely more than half way up betuixt Prestun and Ribcestre, and at ragis of spring tydes farther' he provided the first evidence to be cited in the eighteenth, nineteenth and twentieth century discussions on the likelihood of Ribchester's having been a Roman port.

Momentous events were taking place everywhere at around the time of Leland's visit; nearby, the great abbey of Whalley, six miles away and with great local influence, had been dissolved and its last abbot hanged; the king had become the head of the church in which all worshipped, though few other changes would have been apparent there.

Amidst all this, it is doubtful if the visit of the southern scholar, educated at both our universities and abroad, made much impact.

In any case, few would still have remembered him when, about forty years later, another scholar arrived asking questions – next in a long line stretching to the present day, all brought to this precise spot in the Ribble valley as a result of a Roman officer's appreciation of the landscape in his military view. William Camden, Leland's successor at Ribchester, achieved what Leland did not – publication of a great topographical history of Britain. Schoolmaster and herald, he journeyed throughout the kingdom to research and write, in Latin, his account of *Britannia*. It appeared in 1586, and if ever a writer correctly identified a gap in the market, it must have been Camden. The Latin version of his work went into six editions; it was translated into English by Philemon Holland in 1610; that version, in turn, was reprinted. By the end of the seventeenth century a new edition was issued, newly translated, and edited by Edmund Gibson, and this was reprinted throughout the eighteenth century. Richard Gough's edition of 1789 again updated the work and was itself reissued in 1809, so that it was still the standard national topographical history for the nineteenth century authors.

Camden said of Ribchester, 'where are digged up from time to time so many monuments of Romaine antiquity, statues, pieces of coine, Pillers, Piedistals & Chapters of pillers, heathen altars, Marble stones and inscriptions that the inhabitants may seeme not without cause to have this hobling rhyme arise in their mouthes

> It is written upon a wall in Rome
> Ribchester was as rich as any towne
> in Christendome'.

It was long felt that this might have been evidence of more than proper pride on the part of the Ribchester locals, since it was not so many years since Leland had described the village as a 'poore thing'. The suggestion,

Figure 3. William Camden. Portrait engraved by James Basire from the painting by Marcus Gheeraerts.

made by W. T. Watkin at the end of the nineteenth century, that this 'rhyme' might derive from the partly-misread or mis-remembered inscription on a soldier's discharge *diploma*, seems very reasonable.

Camden recorded the Roman roads to the north and east of the site, calling them the 'port high waies'. He described them as 'raised up with eminent causeis' [causeways], and said of the north road through Bowland Forest that it was 'eminently to be seene for many miles together'. Viewing the inscriptions, the only evidence of the distant past which Camden would have recognised as important, was not a happy experience for him: 'The country folk have so disfigured [them] that although I did see many, yet could I scarcely read one or two of them'. He recorded an altar to Mars and Victory (RIB 585) and the Apollo statue base (RIB 583) at nearby Salesbury Hall in 1582. Another altar, to the Mother Goddesses (RIB 586), he saw only on his second visit in 1603, 'in the house of Thomas Rhodes', as well as a third altar, to Mars the Peacebringer (RIB 584), 'cast out among rubbish stone'. He noted a cavalry tombstone (RIB 595) 'found but the other day', and an elaborate tombstone, erected by a Sarmatian (RIB 594) which 'many yeeres before was found hard by', and which he printed 'Out of William Lambarde's notes'.

The latter was the historian and lawyer whose *Perambulation of Kent* (1576) is the earliest county history known and was intended as the first instalment of a general account of England. Lambarde abandoned this on learning that Camden was engaged on a similar project. Lambarde is probably best known for his *Eirenarcha, or Office of the Justices of the Peace* (1581) and *Archaeion or a Commentary upon the High Court of Justice in England* (1635). In the nineteenth century T. D. Whitaker suggested that Lambarde got his information on this inscription from Laurence Nowell of Read, later Dean of Lichfield. Laurence Nowell was the younger brother of Alexander Nowell, Queen Elizabeth's Dean of St Paul's; Laurence and William Lambarde worked together in the office of another brother, Robert Nowell, attorney, in London.

Camden died in 1623, having retired to the country at least by 1618. It is worth noting that, though he was born in London, his mother was Elizabeth Curwen, daughter of Giles Curwen of Poulton Hall, Lancashire, ultimately descended from the Curwen family of Workington. The Poulton concerned was Poulton-le-Sands, now subsumed in Morecambe.

If the sixteenth century had produced two great topographical historians in Leland and Camden, their legacy in the seventeenth century was far from obvious. While it is true that the middle of the century was bedevilled by that most pernicious of strifes, a civil war, nonetheless much was accomplished in the course of the century in the various arts, and it is sad to find that it was not until 1700 that a book was published which took a serious look at topographical and historical matters in this part of the world, including Ribchester. This was *The Natural History of Lancashire, Cheshire, and the Peak, in Derbyshire: with an account of the British, Phoenician, Armenian, Gr[eek] & Rom[an] Antiquities in those Parts* by Charles Leigh.

Leigh has attracted much opprobrium. The *DNB* said, 'his writings are of little value', and quoted, with approval, T. D. Whitaker on his 'vanity and petulance'. Nevertheless, his statement, at the beginning of his third book, on antiquities, was fairly revolutionary at that date. 'To know what our Ancestors were, cannot be more lively delineated to us, than by the Ruines we discover of those Days; hence it is by penetrating the Bowels of the Earth, we can trace the Footsteps of our Forefathers, and imprint upon our Minds some Idea's of their Times'. And a man who says 'our modern Observations [will] be no small Supplement to the more ancient Ones. Where Mr Cambden and others have saved me the Trouble, I shall fairly name them in order, and in Conclusion add my own' can hardly be accused of plagiarism.

Leigh was a Lancastrian, born at Singleton Grange in the Fylde. He took his B.A. at Brasenose College, Oxford, but left that city in debt and moved to Cambridge, where he graduated M.A. and M.D., having already been elected F.R.S. As a sample of his healthy scepticism and use of scientific means to support it, we may consider his disbelief in the generation of Barnacle Geese from the shell-fish, then widely believed, supporting his argument on sound anatomical grounds.

On archaeological matters, he was prepared to cite the finding of 'Anchors, Rings, and Nails of small Vessels or Boats' at Ribchester, but would not allow that it was ever a port, it being 'at a great Distance from the Ocean and to which there is no River Navigable'. He quoted 'Mr Oddy, School master at Blackburn' at length to the effect that any boats in the area were for crossing the river. Oddy further suggested that the boats were also used on the ditch of the fort, which he saw as having 'a double use viz as a Trench to fortifie the Place, and a Canal (like that up to Holborn Bridge, London)'. Later, Leigh pointed out, what it was to take some time for anyone else to notice, that if water levels were high enough for Ribchester to have been a port, then the Fylde would have been inundated.

Inscriptions were Leigh's weak point, which was to bring his book into academic disfavour later. He was muddled when it came to adding his own observations to those which he quoted from Camden. Thus, on p. 3 he quoted Camden's description of RIB 583, but gave his own description of the stone, without mentioning the inscription, on p. 9. Worst of all, he conflated two inscriptions – RIB 585 and RIB 586 – which he quoted from Camden on pp. 3 and 4, but mixed on p. 8. Strangely, when he came to translate RIB 594, he knew, from Camden, that 'SAR ...' related to the Sarmatians, but took 'ALAE' to be the name of one of them. Nevertheless, his illustrations are better than some which were deemed acceptable nearly 200 years later. Perhaps, as a final instance of Leigh's ability to question accepted ideas, we may note the fact that he refused to believe that Colne was a Roman 'station', pointing out that, while Roman coins had been found there, so they had elsewhere, but that other evidences of Roman settlement such as defences and inscriptions were lacking.

There is some doubt as to the date of Leigh's death, but it came not long after the publication of his book and some years before the appearance of that most important of eighteenth century books in its field, John Horsley's *Britannia Romana* (1732). Horsley is disappointing on Ribchester. Although he said, of RIB 589, 'this is yet in the town', and implied that he saw it and other inscriptions, it is doubtful if he visited the site. He said later, in discussing the route of *Iter X* of the *Antonine Itinerary*, 'In our next stage [i.e. that from Ribchester to Manchester] we are, *according to the intelligence I have received* [my italics], sure of our military way'. Of the site itself he said only, 'I need not describe the Roman station at Ribchester, nor prove

the certainty of it; for it is universally confessed, and the evidences are beyond all exception'. He did, however, note Leigh's confusion of two inscriptions, which is presumably the basis of a rather sour comment to the effect that he had had to rely on Camden, 'having met with little or no assistance from Dr *Leigh's Natural History*'.

One who certainly did come to the site was Dr William Stukeley, travelling through the north with Roger Gale in 1725. He stayed at Ribchester, he tells us, about five hours, and managed to get to both Salesbury and Dinckley Halls, in search of inscriptions. Stukeley devoted some 1700 words to Ribchester, though they did not appear in print until the posthumous publication of the second edition of his *Itinerarium Curiosum* in 1776.

He began by describing the river running 'sonorously' over pebbles and regretted that

Figure 4. Charles Leigh. Portrait from his *Natural History* ... of 1700.

it also ran over Roman remains. He could recognise the outline of the site, and computed it as about 800 feet east to west and 500 feet north to south. He reckoned that the river had eroded about one third of the site. He described various antiquities he was shown – the base of a pillar at the 'Red Lion', a seven-foot shaft with an illegible inscription – and then turned again to the effects of the river. Within living memory, he said, many houses and the chief inn of the village had been washed away. The year previous to that of his visit an orchard had gone, and apple trees could still be seen growing in their own soil where they had fallen at the base of the river bank. Looking at the bank where the fall had occurred, he could see 'the planks and joists of a floor of oak' four feet below the surface. Many of the antiquities of the place had been collected by the late rector, Edward Ogden (rector 1681–1706), but they had been sold by his widow to Mr Prescott of Chester, who was a member of the Prescott family of Ayrefield, Upholland, and an informant of Horsley at Chester. Ogden had been a friend of Leigh and other antiquaries.

Stukeley goes on to describe the west side of the fort, and, at its northern end, Anchor Hill, where he reported the finding of anchors and iron pins for all sizes of ships and barges. He therefore thought the river to have been navigable for smaller vessels. From the northwest angle of the fort he described a road 'of stone like a Roman road' running westwards. Turning eastward again, he described the then current road, called Greengate, which lay on the line of the Roman road over Longridge into Bowland Forest. 'It appears green to the eye', he wrote. Back in the village, he was shown the point, near the 'Red Lion', where a 'subterranean canal', tall enough for a man to stand up in, and stone paved, led into the river. After notes about other finds, including a finger from a statue and two stones from finger-rings, engraved with Mercury, he returned to the matter of the river and the erosion of the bank. In passing,

it may be worth noting that the statue finger and the two ring settings appear in Charles Leigh's plates, and either Stukeley derived them from that source or they were special finds kept at Ribchester to be shown to such visitors as Leigh and Stukeley – perhaps the beginnings of a local museum !

After saying that horses and carriages frequently (!) fell down the river bank where undercutting had narrowed the road, Stukeley added some particulars about nearby finds. He was told of, but did not see, an altar at Panstones (significant name) in Dutton, north of Ribchester. Salesbury and Dinckley he went to, but saw only the Apollo stone (RIB 583), which he described, unlike anyone else to date, as being built into the house itself. He was told that one altar had been taken to Dunkenhalgh (Great Harwood), but others, he thought, to Tabley Old Hall (Cheshire), the other house of the Warren family, who owned Salesbury, Dinckley and Dunkenhalgh.

Although the visit described took place in 1725, by the time an account of it appeared in print, in 1776, more about Ribchester had been published, under the slightly improbable title of *The History of Manchester*, by the Rev. J. Whitaker. This, like so many eighteenth century works, Leigh's and Stukeley's among them, was divided into Books, Book I covering the pre-Roman and Roman periods and Book II the post-Roman. Book I was published first as a quarto volume in 1771. The same material then appeared in two octavo volumes in 1773, and Book II came out as a quarto in 1775.

With Mr Whitaker we really meet the question of the navigability of the Ribble. He had been following Ptolemy's *Geography* up the west coast, and had decided, for what seemed to him to be sufficient reasons, that *Seteia* must have been the river Dee. Given this, he then decided that *Belisama* must have been the Mersey, and that therefore what he called *Portus Sistuntiorum* the Ribble. It must be said that his arguments were based on the sound principles of approximate distances from one point to another, together with the commonsense point that what he called 'the coasting geographer' could not well have missed any of these estuaries. The Ribble he described as admitting ships 'only at the tide of flood, and even then [it] has a navigable channel of an hundred yards in breadth'. This he compared unfavourably with both Mersey and Lune. He then described the way in which the channel of the river was edged 'from Ribchester to the sea' by a 'level of sand, and bordered by a steep bank of earth'. The mouth, he said, was eight or nine miles broad, and 'At such an opening unobstructed by the present sands, the tide would enter with a vast body of water, and flow even up to Ribchester, as it now reaches within six or seven miles of it'. This was then supported by a reference to the 'anchors, rings and nails of small vessels' reported by Leigh.

Whitaker repeated Leigh's idea that the (?western) ditch of the fort connected to the river, and said 'it was clearly a slip, by which at high water a new boat was launched into the Ribble, or an old one brought up from it for reparation'. He went on to say that, had the silting of the Ribble been due to some general geographical factors, the Mersey and Lune would have suffered the same fate. 'It was produced by a cause ... confined ... to the stream of the Ribble. And tradition, the faithful preserver of many a fact which history has overlooked or forgotten, speaks consistently of such a cause, ascribing the final ruin of Ribchester to the overwhelming violence of an earthquake'.

To turn from these flights of fancy, which I suspect Dr Leigh might have viewed a little sceptically, Whitaker set about collating his documentary and his archaeological evidence. He knew of a Roman site at Ribchester; he had decided that *Portus Sistuntiorum* (as his corrupt text of Ptolemy's *Geography* called it) was at the mouth of the Ribble; and he had another text which gave him a named site (*Reriogonum*) in the right

direction and at the right distance from the Ribble mouth. This text was the *Itinerary of Richard of Cirencester*. Now long exposed as a forgery, the importance of this lies in its influence on topographical historians between the date of its publication and that of its discreditation, and we must pause briefly to explore its story (See Randall 1933).

Charles Bertram was born in London in 1723, moved to Copenhagen in 1743, and obtained a licence to teach English to naval cadets there. In 1747 he began a correspondence with Dr William Stukeley, in the course of which he casually mentioned a manuscript owned by a friend of his. This purported to be a history of Britain – *de Situ Britanniae* – the surviving portions of which were a geographical description of the islands, an itinerary of Roman roads and a map. Stukeley was hooked by the bait, obtained a sample of the handwriting, which the then keeper of the Cottonian Library pronounced to be of the fourteenth century, a transcript of the text and a copy of the map. These together, Stukeley said, added as many as 175 names of sites in Roman Britain which were new or had been wrongly placed previously.

Bertram was lucky. One or two of his guesses at sites turned out to be right, which suggested to some people that the author of the manuscript possessed knowledge which had not otherwise come to light. Even his choice of name for his author was lucky. 'Richard of Westminster', his original name, was a safe bet. Westminster Abbey was large enough to be certain to have included a Richard among its monks within the right period. What Bertram did not at first know was that a real Westminster monk called Richard *did* write a chronicle, *Speculum Historiale*, in the fourteenth century. As soon as Stukeley made this clear to Bertram, his 'author' became 'Ricardus Corinensis'. He had no means of knowing that the real Richard called himself 'Ricardus Cirencestriensis'.

Stukeley published Bertram's forgery in 1757, and John Whitaker was among the first to make extensive use of it. To his credit, T. D. Whitaker (no relation) of whom we shall have much to say in the next chapter, was among the earliest sceptics. Although thoroughly exposed in 1870, 'Richard' was still being quoted throughout the nineteenth century.

John Whitaker was ahead of his time in one respect. He envisaged, admittedly on the evidence of probability only, a 'town' and a 'fortress' at Ribchester as separate entities. To be sure, he felt it necessary to postulate the 'town' only because of his views on the navigability of the Ribble. On this subject, further consideration led him to place the Roman sea-port at Freckleton, where he described the port of Preston to have been in his own day, and to imagine that 'The exports of the neighbouring districts would be carried to Ribchester, lodged in the warehouses of the town, and sent in boats to the vessels in the harbour' [and *vice versa*].

Of the site of Ribchester itself he said little. 'The Ribble has been almost the only dis- coverer of antiquities. And as it yearly bears down the bank of the town, and transfers a part of the site to the southern margin of the current, the floorings and foundations of houses have been visible in the face of the bank, and about two or three feet below the surface of it' and 'Great have been the encroachments which the river has made upon the town, within these sixty years only. One whole street of houses, and a range of orchards and gardens, have been carried away by the stream'.

The next important event in the investiga- tion of the Roman site at Ribchester occurred in 1796, with the discovery of the parade hel- met and its associated finds. This is fully discussed in Chapter 8, so we can pass on now to the last of the eighteenth century visitors.

He was Thomas Pennant, and his obser- vations were published in *A Tour from Downing to Alston Moor* in 1801. Pennant is perhaps best known to readers as one of the

two principal correspondents of Gilbert White of Selborne, the other being Daines Barrington. Pennant was born and lived at Downing in the parish of Whitford, near Holywell, in Flintshire. He had carried out a tour in Ireland, and published a four-volume *British Zoology*, together with his first tour, in Scotland, before he undertook the tour with which we are concerned. According to the (anonymous) editor who prepared the posthumous publication, this tour took place in 1773, and Pennant was accompanied by the artist Moses Griffith.

Figure 5. Memorial to Thomas Pennant at Whitford Church, Flintshire.

Figure 6. Thomas Dunham Whitaker. Portrait on ivory at Whalley Church. (By courtesy of the Rev. C. Sterry, vicar.)

The route of the tour was probably determined mainly by the availability of places to stay. It ran from Flintshire to Chester, thence north-east to Warrington, with a diversion to Warburton, north-west to Sefton, then north-east through Lancashire to Clitheroe. The route then continued north-east to Malham, and then north-west to Kendal; a great loop then took them through Kirkby Stephen, Brough and Penrith, north and across Hadrian's Wall to Bewcastle, and finally in a westward loop through Burgh-by-Sands and Carlisle and eventually to Alston. Their return through Harrogate was published separately. At only two places on the western tour did they stop for more than one night and carry out excursions. One of these was at Standen Hall, near Clitheroe, where their host was John Aspinall, and whence they went on one trip to Mitton, Stonyhurst, Bashall Hall and Waddington. The other trip was to Whalley, Langho, Hacking Hall, Salesbury and Ribchester.

Pennant says he came to Ribchester over the New Bridge, 'an elegant structure of three elliptical arches'. This immediately raises problems because of the history of the bridges near Ribchester. Stukeley had referred to 'a noble bridge of four very large arches, lately built by the country', but this had been replaced by a five-arched structure which was barely finished when it was washed away, before the horrified eyes of the bridge superintendent, in the great flood of October, 1771, which also destroyed all the bridges on the Tyne with the sole exception of Corbridge Bridge. At Ribchester (or rather, near it, for 'Ribchester Bridge' has never been in Ribchester in the last three hundred years, but about half a mile higher up the river) the contract for the new, three-arched bridge was not signed until 1775, and the bridge was completed the following year. It does not seem possible to reconcile the alleged date of Pennant's tour with his having crossed the bridge he describes, and one can only assume that details were updated before publication (see Edwards 1994).

Pennant described the depredations of the river in terms which are now familiar, and said that nothing of the Roman site was to be seen on the ground 'except the rampart and foss near the church'. He saw RIB 589, and what was presumably RIB 592. He also saw RIB 583 at Salesbury, and the relief of the standard bearer which is still at Standen Hall, and which had been found in digging a grave in Ribchester churchyard. He quoted Leigh's conflation of RIB 585 and 586, referring only to Camden and Horsley, and described RIB 586 fully. He knew of Leigh's book, for he quoted it on other finds, and he also described a finger-ring with the inscription AVE MEA VITA, which John Aspinall had seen 'in the possession of a poor man'. The remainder of Pennant's comments relate to the old questions of the port, the level of the tides and so forth.

Pennant began his contribution to this debate by suggesting that the function of the

Roman fort at Ribchester had been to protect the upper end of the 'Setantiorum Portus, the estuary of the Ribble'. Here, he was anticipating his conclusion that 'a tide, in the time of the Romans, and probably long after, flowed over the whole plain, near as high as Salesbury. It had apparently been an estuary'. He then produced two cards which, if not quite trumps, he evidently thought of as picture cards. First, of Anchor Hill, he recorded anchors and rings of ships 'and even a ship itself. This was discovered about twelve years ago, by sinking a well for a pump. Its dimensions are not known, nor can they be found without pulling down some building with which part is now covered'. Secondly, he produced a calculation. Leland, somewhere between 1536 and 1542, saw the tide flow half way between Preston and Ribchester. In his own time, 240 years later, the highest it came was two miles above Preston. The implication, not clearly stated, was that if the highest tidal point had retreated three miles in 240 years, then the river must have been tidal at Ribchester in Roman times. If the calculation was really that simple, the tide would, in fact, have reached somewhere about Hellifield in Roman times! Pennant then went on to quote J. Whitaker on the probable Roman port of Freckleton, hedging his bets somewhat by saying, 'probably no very large ships ever came up as high as Ribchester'.

It is amusing and instructive to see how two factors have inspired and maintained this entirely unnecessary argument right down to the present day – the name Anchor Hill, for which there is a perfectly good alternative explanation (see p. 38), and the flat-bottomed 'western' ditch of the fort, which ended abruptly at the river's edge as a result of erosion.

CHAPTER THREE

Work in the Nineteenth Century

When we come to the nineteenth century in following the study of the Roman site at Ribchester, we immediately encounter a figure who had a tremendous influence on the writing of the history of Lancashire, Thomas Dunham Whitaker. The Whitaker family had lived at the Holme, in the Yorkshire border parish of Cliviger, from medieval times, but Thomas was born, in 1759, at Rainham in Norfolk, where his father was the parson. The following year, however, the family returned to the ancestral home in Lancashire, and Thomas was educated, first by a tutor in Rochdale, and then, after a bout of illness, by the Rev. William Sheepshanks at Grassington. Sheepshanks had been Fellow and Tutor of St John's College, Cambridge, and it is probably due to him that Whitaker became a member of that College. He took the degree of Ll.B. in 1781, but the death of his father in 1782 prevented his entering his expected career in the law. He returned to Cliviger and was ordained deacon and priest in the following year. He then spent the considerable sum (for the late eighteenth century) of £400 in recovering the family patronage of the living of Holme Chapel. Then, in 1797, he presented himself to the living. It is, perhaps, as well to recall that this was perfectly legal, and, indeed, normal for a landed family at that time, though it was more common for a son, often a younger son, to be presented to the family living.

Whitaker, of course, became a celebrated topographical historian, his first book being *A History ... of the Ancient Parish of Whalley*. Interestingly, the publication of this book (in 1800–1801) preceded his becoming vicar of Whalley by some nine years. He remained vicar of Whalley until his death in 1822, combining this from 1813 to 1819 with the rectory of Heysham and, from 1818 to his death, with the vicarage of Blackburn. Again, neither the holding of a number of church benefices at the same time, nor his residence elsewhere, was in any way unusual. The duties of the churches were performed by assistant curates for whose recruitment and remuneration Whitaker himself would have been responsible.

Whalley was a very large ancient parish indeed, covering 106,395 acres or over 166 square miles, and containing some 47 townships. Adjacent to it was Ribchester, and in the Roman past of that village Whitaker became greatly interested. The text relating to Ribchester in the first edition of *Whalley* was entirely derivative from earlier workers, but it was while he was preparing this book that a very important discovery was made at Ribchester. This was the parade helmet and its associated objects, found in 1796, and described fully in Chapter 8 below. Whitaker's involvement in this was almost certainly crucial. He was a gregarious man, though sometimes described as shy.

An example of the former quality is the fact that he organised a kind of discussion group for local clergy and others, and there is no doubt that he was closely involved with the local gentry. Gentry himself, and a magistrate for both Lancashire and Yorkshire, he was well acquainted with Charles Townley of Towneley Hall, part of the park of which actually fell within Cliviger, wherein also lay the Holme. It was the friendship with Townley, very much a member of London society, which secured for Whitaker the services of

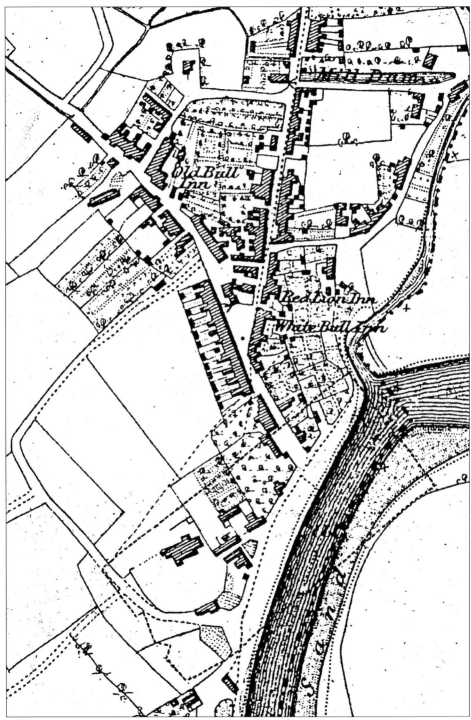

Figure 7. The village as shown on the first six–inch Ordnance Survey map, 1845. What was then thought to be the outline of the fort is indicated by dotted lines. The north-south dimension is not greatly wrong, but the east-west is too great by about a third. Reproduced from the 1st edition 1845 Ordnance Survey Map.

the young J. M. W. Turner to provide illustrations for *Whalley*. Naturally, then, when a remarkable discovery was made at Ribchester, Whitaker knew of it and informed Townley, collector of classical antiquities, about it. In fact, of course, the helmet and other items lay a little outside Townley's normal collecting range, but nevertheless he bought and published them. Probably, but for Whitaker's interest, they would never have come to Townley's notice.

Townley's publication of the Ribchester items, in the Society of Antiquaries' folio serial *Vetusta Monumenta* was not completed until 1800, and it was probably knowledge of the imminent appearance of this which prevented Whitaker from including a description of the find in his *Whalley*. He did, however, rather curiously, engage James Basire, who had drawn and engraved most of the objects for Townley, to perform the same function for him. Thus, two plates of the Ribchester finds (plus one or two other items) appeared in the first (1800–1801), second (1808) and third (1816) editions of *Whalley*, but without any accompanying text. This was supplied, fifty years after Whitaker's death, by the editors of the fourth (1872–1876) edition.

At the time of the writing of *Whalley*, Whitaker was inclined to believe that Ribchester had been a Roman port, and argued that the changes in the relative level implied by this could be explained without the intervention of the earthquake inferred by his namesake, John. T. D. wrote again of Ribchester in *Richmondshire*, published in 1823–1825, and by then pointed out that the port theory would have required the drowning of much of the Fylde, though he would probably not have admitted that Charles Leigh had made the same point over a century earlier.

A more significant advance made by Whitaker was to attribute the building of the fort to Agricola, and this, not seriously doubted for another hundred and fifty years, solely from a critical reading of Tacitus. The sophisticated ability of the modern archaeologist to date such items as pottery was not available to him.

Equally pioneering was Whitaker's organisation of the first known excavation on the site to be carried out specifically in pursuit of knowledge. An inscribed stone, broken and re-used, face down, as a paving stone (RIB 587) had been found in 1811 in the river bank. In 1813, Whitaker excavated on the site of what we now know as the garrison commander's house (*praetorium*). By chance we know that the 1811 inscription was found by one Adam Cottam, because an inscribed stone, which was evidently its label when it was displayed somewhere locally, was recovered a few years ago from the garden of the de Tabley Arms, across Ribchester Bridge. The inscription reads: 'This Stone taken/ out of ye Foundation/ of a *ROMAN* TEMPLE/ at RIBCHESTER/ By A: Cottam 1811'.

Cottam (1755–1838) is an intriguing character. He is said to have been a surveyor, and was certainly agent to the Bradyll family, of Portfield, Whalley, in which post he followed his father, Richard. Adam is said to have 'raised from obscurity as his pupil' John Barrow, later to be Secretary of the Admiralty and to be knighted. Barrow was born at Ulverston, and the likely connection is the Bradyll family, who had land nearby, including Conishead Priory. Whether from his duties as an agent or from other undiscovered sources, Cottam made money. He was a generous benefactor to Whalley, where his almshouses can still be seen. So, too, can the stone gateways to the churchyard for which he paid, the organ, discarded by the Priory church at Lancaster, and the painting of *The Agony in the Garden* by Northcote, both of which he bought for the church. Cottam was an executor of Whitaker's will, and his own was witnessed by Robert Nowell Whitaker, Thomas's son and successor as vicar of Whalley.

Whitaker, as might be expected, had obviously spent some time talking to the villagers at Ribchester, and he recorded one local legend of some interest. The villagers described the finding of the skull of an ox covered in leather and studded with gold. Apart, obviously, from the absence of horns, there is no great distinction, to the eye of a layman, between the skull of an ox and that of a horse, and one is tempted to see in this story memories of the discovery of the skull of a horse complete with its leather *chamfron*, like those found in this century at Newstead and *Vindolanda*. The kind of waterlogged conditions which would have preserved the leather, and which are met with almost everywhere in lower levels at Ribchester, would also have preserved the bronze rivets with which the *chamfron* was decorated without corrosion and therefore looking like gold. The probability of this interpretation was still further increased by the finding, in the most recent large-scale excavations at Ribchester, of parts of two *chamfrons*.

Any advances in understanding which Whitaker contributed in his day are likely to have been superseded by more recent developments. One activity of his for which we must always be grateful, however, was the acquisition of five of the inscribed stones from the site. A specific provision in his will bequeathed these to the Master and Fellows of his old college, St John's, Cambridge, and it is by the enlightened consent of their successors that we see these in the site Museum* today, where they were deposited on loan in 1967.

Whitaker died in 1821, at the age of 62. There is a tendency to think of the venerable doctor (Whitaker became D.C.L. in 1801) writing his great series of *Histories*, but he was only 41 years of age at the time of the appearance of *Whalley*. The next county historian to build upon Whitaker's foundations was Edward Baines. He published his *History*

of the Duchy and County Palatine of Lancaster in 1831–32. This summarised the current state of knowledge about Ribchester. For his second editon of 1836, Baines was able to add one significant discovery, made in 1833 by the Rev. S. J. Allen of Salesbury, namely that of the altar for the health and victory of Caracalla and Julia Domna (RIB 590).

This was found in the churchyard, though no indication is given of how or why the incumbent of Salesbury was digging in Ribchester churchyard. Mr Allen was later to describe steps, found at the same time as the altar, which were almost certainly the steps of the *principia* strongroom.

That Ribchester was beginning to be widely regarded as an important Roman site is evident from the next event of note in the investigation of its past. In 1850, members of the British Archaeological Association, meeting in Manchester and Lancaster, made an excursion to the site. As often on such occasions, an excavation had been laid on for them. This was under the superintendence of John Harland, who was to edit a third edition of Baines's work in 1868, and John Just. The excavation exposed part of the south-west wall of the fort, and was reported, together with a summary of the current knowledge about Roman Ribchester, in the Association's *Journal* for 1850. The report, however, was scarcely exhaustive, consisting of the following: 'The excavations lately undertaken with the view of obtaining information for this congress, have laid bare the outer wall to its foundations on the western side. Unlike the foundations of the ramparts at Borrow Bridge, Melandra Castle, etc., it consists of loose stones, without mortar, or the cement grouting common to such foundations'.

Despite Harland's editorship, the third edition of Baines's work had nothing of note to add, and indeed little was to change until the last two decades of the century. One exception to this came with the discovery, in 1876, of the second-best-known object from the site. This was the cavalryman's

---

* This is the first time that the Museum has been mentioned. Its story is recounted in Chapter 7.

tombstone, found apparently washed out of the left bank of the river upstream of the fort. This is presumably evidence for the siting of at least one cemetery, but the piece, which is fully described in Chapter 9, is odd in that it does not have an inscription. One can only assume that the inscription was on a separate piece of stone. There is scarcely room on the piece itself for even a painted inscription.

The next landmark comes with the publication of W. Thompson Watkin's *Roman Lancashire* in 1883. This volume brought together almost everything which was known about its subject in 1883, and Watkin missed little. It was, therefore, and remains, a very useful quarry, but the nature of the evidence which Watkin cites, as much for Ribchester as for other places, is interesting. It is almost wholly concerned with objects, and shows even less concern for evidence on the ground than do some of its predecessors. In fact, when Watkin ventured into originality, he was demonstrably inaccurate. Having dismissed Stukeley's estimate of the proportion of the fort site eroded by the river, he proceeded to his own estimate of its size, which was 300 yards in one direction and 135 yards in the other. 'Assuming the other sides to be of somewhat similar dimensions', he wrote, 'the area of the *castrum* would be about ten acres'. This is somewhat curious, because the calculation is a simple one and the result is just over eight and one third acres.

Watkin's treatment of the site, which is largely reprinted from his paper on the subject published in 1878, is admirably logical. He records the antiquarian references, such as Leland, Camden, Stukeley, he deals with the inscriptions; he enumerates finds recorded, including some then or now not to be found; he deals with the helmet and its associated material; he lists seventeen coins (only) of 'a very large quantity found at the station ... (and) so rapidly dispersed that the number traceable is even less than at Manchester'.

Attention has been drawn to the small concern shown, by such writers as Just and

Harland or Watkin, about evidence in, or even on, the ground. Back in the early years of the century, Whitaker had dug at Ribchester in order to obtain evidence, and although he was not concerned with such matters as stratigraphy or even plan, his interest did go beyond the mere recovery of artefacts. By contrast, the 1850 excavations for the Archaeological Congress were clearly carried out only to provide a curiosity for the delegates to stare at. With these facts in mind we can see that the excavations carried out in 1888–1889 were momentous. For the first time an attempt was made to lay out excavations with a view to the recovery of specific knowledge – in this case the outline plan of the fort. Their cost was met from two sources, the Rev. J. Shortt, vicar of Hoghton, and the *Preston Herald*. We may presume that Shortt had some say in the layout, and the excavations were credited to him when the report appeared as part of *The History of the Parish of Ribchester*, published in 1890 and written by Shortt and Tom C. Smith. There is, however, at least a suggestion that 'the man on the ground' may have had something to do with the siting of the trenches.

He was James Bertwistle, Architect, of Blackburn. He is not named in Smith and Shortt's book, but his original drawings were preserved (and, at one time, exhibited) in the Museum. The drawings were signed by Bertwistle, who described himself as above, and added 'under whose supervision the excavations were carried out', a careful and firm attribution which might be thought to hint at some tension between the sponsor of the excavations and the director in the field. This idea is somewhat reinforced by a discrepancy. Smith and Shortt describe and plot seven trenches excavated in 1888 and an eighth, said to have been cut in December, 1889 [*sic*]. Of this latter, they wrote 'By an unfortunate misunderstanding, for which neither of the writers is responsible, no sketch was made of section No. 8'. This latter is said to have been in the western angle of the fort,

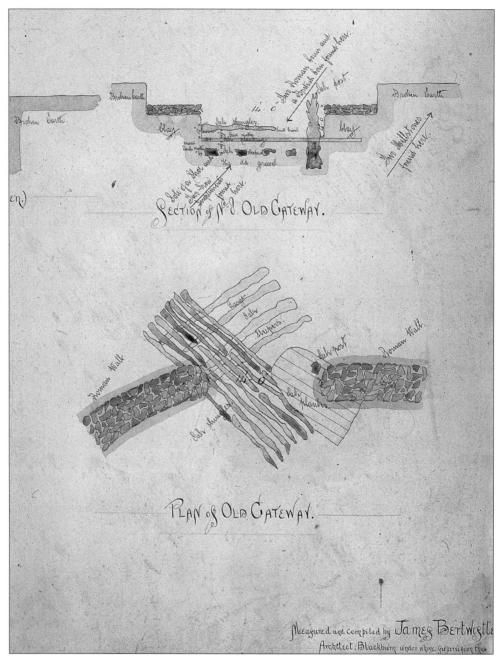

Figure 8. Plan of excavation of the defences of the north corner of the fort, 1883. Drawn by James Bertwistle.

and to have revealed there a 'gateway similar to that discovered in the northern corner'. However, Bertwistle's original drawings are dated December, 1888, show seven trenches on the plan and a detailed plan of the alleged *northern* gateway as trench No. 8.

It is a measure of the fact, which we may find difficult to remember over a century later, that there was no tradition of Romano-British excavation at the time, that the next excavator to tackle Ribchester was an Oxford undergraduate reading mathematics, ultimately to become a distinguished exponent of Egyptian archaeology. John Garstang was the son of a Blackburn doctor, and worked in Ribchester in 1898 and 1899 under the auspices of the Ribchester Excavation Fund. His interest in the site is said to have been aroused during schoolboy trips from Blackburn to the observatory at Stonyhurst College. It was his Ribchester work which caused Francis Haverfield to recommend him to take up archaeology, and thus led to his long-lasting career in middle eastern archaeology. It was, indeed, probably Haverfield who first suggested that he excavate at Ribchester.

Garstang's first report was short, but made a respectable pamphlet; his second was even shorter, consisting only of a single folded sheet. He plotted the results of previous work, including the seven 1888 trenches and the alleged northern gateway. In the western corner of the fort on his plan is a clear indication of the corner tower we would expect there. In the southern corner is another, provided with a very large drain. The gap in the stone wall overlying the timber strapping at the north corner, found in 1888, together with the large drain, dubbed 'tunnel', at the south, are the cause of the unlikely attempts, made at this time, to endow the fort with corner gateways. One might have thought that the attempt to draw one of these in restoration for the cover of the 1898 report would have demonstrated their near impossibility. One can only assume that the unfortunate artist had to do his best, as to admit that the corner gateways made no sense would have necessitated the rewriting of a substantial part of the report!

It was Garstang, too, who plotted, presumably on the basis of Whitaker's verbal description, the find-spot of the 1796 helmet hoard at a point on the river bank more or less opposite the door of the Museum as it

Figure 9. John Garstang. Portrait at Queen Elizabeth's Grammar School, Blackburn. (By courtesy of the Headmaster)

was constructed a few years later. More usefully, the 1899 work had just begun to reveal fragments of the headquarters building and the granaries, though they were not understood. But despite the plans and the attempted reconstruction drawings, it was still 'relics' which really interested people at that date, as a glance at Garstang's plate will show.

There was, apparently some sort of crisis not long after this. The 1898 and 1899 reports appeared under the heading of the Ribchester Excavation Fund. The first of these claimed that eight named persons, five of them M.P.s, were patrons. The second enumerates no fewer than ten individuals as patrons, amongst whom are only two of the previous year's eight. To these are added the Society of Antiquaries of London, the two joint Lancashire and Cheshire societies and the Burnley Literary and Scientific Club. However, there was set up in 1900 a Ribchester Excavation Fund Committee. This agreed to an aim of raising up to £200 for the continuance of excavation at Ribchester. Garstang attended its first meeting, in May, under the chairmanship of Bertwistle, whom we previously saw directing the 1888 excavations. At the Committee's second meeting, in July, the Secretary was instructed to write to Garstang dissenting from an agreement made between him and the Rev. R. Harries, the Rector. He was also to deplore the making of independent agreements of this kind without the Committee's assent. To Mr Harries, the Secretary was to repeat these last sentiments and to request that a deputation from the Committee be allowed to meet him to discuss future excavation.

At its third meeting the Committee repeated much of what had been agreed at the previous meeting and carefully repudiated responsibility for any expenditure incurred other than with its agreement. The fourth meeting merely arranged to hold a special meeting in September, at which it was agreed that the Committee would take over the accounts of the Ribchester Excavation Fund and that the whole Committee should be appointed as a deputation to meet Harries. The report of that meeting was submitted at the Committee's meeting in October, and it is clear that little progress had been made. A discussion on further action was deferred. Nothing is then recorded for seven months, by which time it was reported that a letter had been received from Harries conveying a number of complaints for which the Committee said they could not take responsibility as they were not in existence at the material time. Four months then passed, and the Committee met finally in November, 1901, and dissolved itself. The eighth and last meeting, incidentally, was the only one, apart from the first, at which Garstang was present. A newspaper report at the time makes it clear that it was lack neither of enthusiasm nor of funds which curtailed activity, but the impossibility of securing an agreement with the rector.

CHAPTER FOUR

Twentieth-Century Excavations

In the twentieth century progress was more rapid, and the account will necessarily be somewhat more summary. In 1902, Garstang published a list of Roman remains from Ribchester, which consisted largely of carved and/or inscribed stones. There were a few references to 'ornaments' and a list of 73 coins. At the same time he made a disastrous attempt to reconstruct a temple within the fort. Whitaker had tried to do the same nearly a hundred years earlier, and on this Garstang was scathing. 'The restoration suggested by

Dr Whitaker', he wrote, '... would have placed there a structure hardly less imposing than the Parthenon itself'. He himself then took the following 'evidence': fragments of the *praetorium* excavated in 1813; five column bases, of which one was described by Stukeley in 1725, three were at the Rectory and one at Lower Alston Farm; a stone lion; the columns supporting the portico of the Stydd alms-houses; Whitaker's temple inscription (RIB 587); the parade helmet; and the 1833 altar for the health and victory of Caracalla and Julia

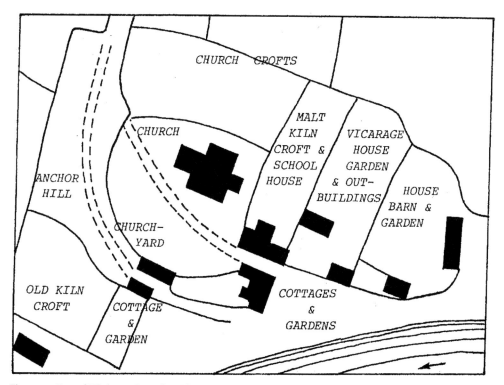

Figure 10. Part of Ribchester from the Tithe Award, 1838. (Lancashire Record Office DRB 1/164) The 'Cottages and Gardens' are what became Churchgates, while 'Malt Kiln Croft and Schoolhouse' indicates the predecessor of the Parish Hall.

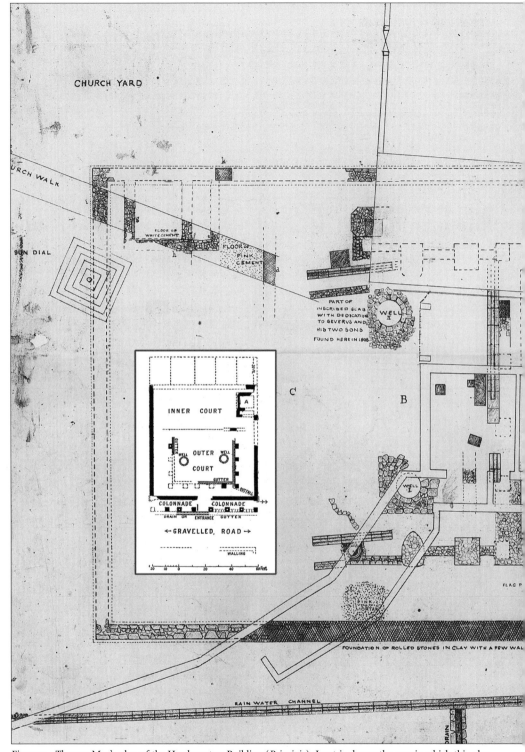

Figure 11. Thomas May's plan of the Headquarters Building (*Principia*). Inset is shown the way in which this plan was 'pruned' for *Roman Britain in 1914*.

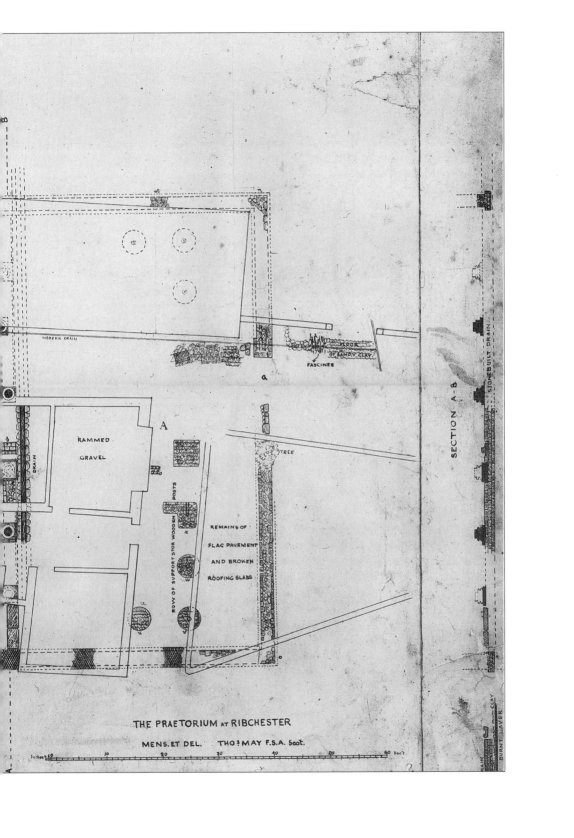

THE PRAETORIUM AT RIBCHESTER

MENS. ET DEL.   THOS MAY F.S.A. Scot.

Domna (RIB 590). From this hotch-potch, with a wealth of classical learning, he concluded 'that the temple at Ribchester was Prostyle and of the Roman Doric order, about 25 feet wide by 50 feet in length'. It was Francis Haverfield who pointed out, gently but firmly, in the following year that 'temples have no place in Roman forts'.

A different spirit was abroad soon after this, and the name on which all turns is Greenall. Miss Margaret Greenall is credited, on an inscription within it, with the foundation of the Museum at Ribchester. Her part in this is examined in Chapter 7, but her earlier actions are at least as significant for the exploration of the site. She had bought a group of cottages just outside the churchyard and close to the river. These were ultimately to be turned into the house still called Churchgates, but Miss Greenall's great idea was to allow the complete excavation of the area occupied by the house and its surroundings, as rebuilding took place. To carry out the work she brought in a new name to Ribchester – Thomas May. The point of contact for these various strands was Warrington.

Miss Greenall was a member of the family whose great brewery was sited on and around the Roman settlement at Wilderspool, just outside Warrington, where, as I write, the archaeological opportunities presented by the demolition of that brewery are beginning to be realised. May, born in Cambridge in 1842, had been educated at Edinburgh. He had come, as supervisor of Inland Revenue, to Warrington, and had retired there in 1903. From 1895 to 1905 he had excavated at the Wilderspool site and now, in November, 1906, he began work at Ribchester. Between 12 November, 1906 and 13 May, 1908 he spent a total of just over seventeen weeks excavating at Ribchester. Some of his notebooks survive, full of plans, sections and drawings of objects, all with dimensions added in red ink. In addition, there are many pages of notes on specific subjects which show that his reading was wide and by no means confined to British material. Also surviving are his plan of the headquarters building as he excavated it and of the central range of buildings northwest of it, where he also worked, joined in 1908 by G. L. Cheesman and, for a time, by J. J. Phelps. It is worth emphasising, incidentally, what a pioneering, innovative and near-unique piece of rescue archaeology his work at Churchgates was, long before that expression had been invented.

In 1911, the Ribchester Excavation Committee issued, under the editorship of their secretary, J. H. Hopkinson, what he called 'a brief statement of the present position'. He explained that full reports on the excavations had been written by May and Cheesman; that the latter had also dealt with the garrison and with the inscriptions; plans and photographs had been prepared and Professor Dobson of Bristol had written on Roman Place Names in Lancashire. Hopkinson went on: 'It was hoped … that all … might be included in a volume dealing in detail with the whole question of Roman Ribchester. That hope is still deferred owing to legal and other delays'. Poor Hopkinson would presumably have been somewhat horrified had he known that this hope would never be fulfilled in the form in which he imagined it, and that it would be approaching the new millennium before the texts to which he referred, and which still exist, could be taken into consideration in the present, somewhat different, work.

Two inter-related ideas then arose. First, the feeling grew that there ought to be a museum on the site at Ribchester; and, second, that the building of it ought to be integrated with the demolition of the existing schoolroom and its replacement by a new Parish Room and Museum. Since the schoolroom lay on the site of the remainder of the headquarters building not already excavated by May, there was an obvious opportunity, indeed necessity, for further excavation. Attempts were made to persuade Thomas May to return, but he had left Warrington for

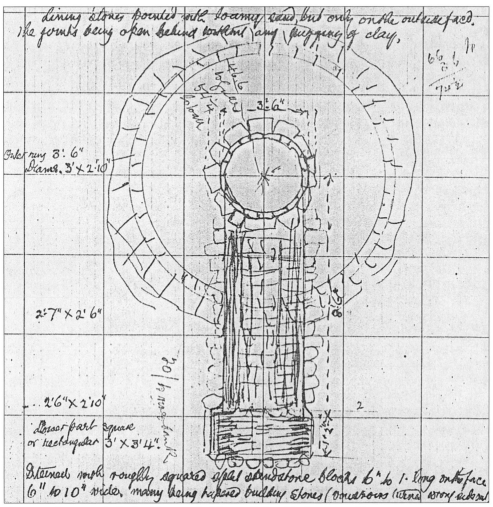

Figure 12. Thomas May's sketch of the second of three wells found in the course of the 1906–1908 excavations. This one, found on 11 April, 1907, was 9′ 8″ deep. The notes reproduced read 'Lining stones pointed with loamy sand, but only on the outside face, the joints being open behind without any pugging of clay. Steined with roughly squared sandstone blocks 6″ to 1′ long on the face, 6″ to 10″ wide, many being tapered building stones (voussoirs turned wrong side out)'. This well had its lower part square or rectangular and lined with oak timbers. The first well, found 13–14 November, 1906, was 10′ 6″ deep, and the third, 10′ deep and found 27 April, 1908, had the capitals from the *principia* in its filling.

Crieff in Perthshire, and could not be persuaded. When the somewhat drawn-out negotiations for the demolition of the old building and its replacement by new were concluded, and the schoolroom was demolished in 1914, it was Donald Atkinson, Research Fellow of Reading College, who excavated.

The Museum was opened in 1915, as described in Chapter 7, and a second edition of Hopkinson's pamphlet was issued in 1916. The Great War, which had not gone unremarked at the opening ceremony of the new Museum, now further touched Ribchester, for the 1916 edition of *The Roman Fort at Ribchester* opened with a memorial dedication to Lieut. G. L. Cheesman, Hampshire Regiment, killed at Suvla Bay in 1915. *The Auxilia of the Roman Imperial Army* (1914) hints at what was thereby lost to Romano-British scholarship.

It was another twelve years before the third, and final, edition of Hopkinson's work was issued, this time under the editorship of Donald Atkinson, by now Reader in Ancient History at Manchester University. It, too, opened with a memorial dedication, this time to Margaret Greenall. Just as the memorial dedications and the changing status of Atkinson highlight passing incidentals in the story of Roman Ribchester, so the three editions of Hopkinson's pamphlet show him changing from Lecturer in Classical Archaeology at Manchester University to Vicar of Colne and, finally, to Inspector of Education, Diocese of Carlisle.

The new edition recorded work by Atkinson in 1920 outside the 'north' (=NW) gate and in 1921 in the Rectory grounds, but its plan was totally unaltered from that of 1916. This plan, in turn, had been little different from that of 1911, with one interesting and important exception. In 1911, May had shown the *principia* extending across the line of the *via principalis*, as is shown in his manuscript plans, because that is what he excavated. In the 1916 edition of the plan, this part of the *principia* has been removed, with the exception of the colonnade in the front of the building, which has also been supplied with a hypothetical, though presumably certain , rear range of five rooms in dotted lines. This change can be traced back to a piece of intellectual chicanery, for in Haverfield's *Roman Britain in 1914*, the *principia* is similarly pruned.

One is forced to the conclusion that the archaeological establishment, as represented by Haverfield, Camden Professor of Ancient History in the University of Oxford, could do this to Thomas May, retired tax official, and get away with it. One wonders what May's reaction was. The explanation given in

Figure 13. The threshold of the eastern guardchamber of the north gate, as excavated by Thomas May. The stone has obviously been re-used.

the text is that 'excavations in 1906–7, however, left the size and extent of these remains somewhat uncertain and resulted in what we now know to be an incorrect plan'. In practice, this means that one either believes May's plan of the *principia* as he excavated it, or one does not. He had understood the extension when he excavated it, being aware of continental parallels. Not only did May locate the bases of the south-eastern half of the north-eastern colonnade of the forehall, but he located the northern and eastern corners of the building, together with parts of its south-eastern wall and a fragment of its north-western wall. To dismiss all this airily as 'incorrect' without quoting further evidence is somewhat high-handed. There was no British example of such a forehall known when May was excavating, but by the time Haverfield wrote, the Newstead 'entrance hall', as Curle named it, was in print.

Both May and Curle (and, of course, Haverfield) knew of such buildings in Germany, where they are relatively common (the

Figure 14. Four photographs of the demolition of the Sunday School in 1914. The first shows that the remains of the *principia* were barely below the floor level. The second shows a column base actually under the south wall. This was immediately below the two windows seen in the first photograph. These are on the north wall of Churchgates. The third and fourth photographs show a rectangular foundation at the west end of the Sunday School Room. It may well have been the firing chamber of the malt kiln referred to as preceding the Sunday School.

four British examples known now join 27 or more on the continent, mostly in Germany and *Raetia*). In Germany they are known as *exerzierhalle*; but it was Sir Mortimer Wheeler who excavated that at Brecon Gaer and connected such buildings with the Netherby inscription (RIB 978) which refers to a *basilica equestris exercitatoria*, that is, loosely, a cavalry exercise hall. The only remarkable feature of the Ribchester forehall is that it seems to have been no wider than the *principia* itself; but although this is not true of the other three British examples, there are parallels in Germany. By contrast, Haverfield's retention of the colonnade nearest to the *principia* did produce an unusual situation, for which he could quote only the unpublished example at Caersws as a parallel.

Whatever the relationship between the archaeological establishment and May, he too, eventually joined it, being elected Fellow of the Society of Antiquaries in 1916, receiving an honorary degree from Manchester University in 1919 and writing, among other

Figure 15. The excavators of the remains below the Sunday School. The following have been identified. Back row: 1.? Murray; 2. – ; 3. Richard Barton (later the first custodian of the Museum); 4.? Kenyon; 5. – ; Middle row: 1. Wally Bennett; 2. – ; 3. James Eccles; In front: John Hallows, Stockton Heath, Thomas May's foreman in 1906–1908. (Courtesy of Mrs Ena Jones)

things, important accounts of the Roman pottery from Colchester and Silchester, as well as dealing with the pottery from the Richborough excavations.

To return for a moment to the *principia*, Atkinson notes that 'in 1925 the opportunity offered by the restoration of the sundial in the churchyard was used to test the correctness of Professor Haverfield's hypothesis'. This had been that the rear of the *principia* lay about twenty feet back from where May had drawn it. Atkinson says, 'The continuation of the east wall of his [i.e. Haverfield's] suggested rear range of rooms was discovered and a return wall on its west side within a few inches of the suggested line of the south wall of his northernmost room. Thus the existence of the range of rooms and the N-S dimension of the northernmost are proved, but the evidence as to the western end of the south granary suggests that his E-W dimension is a little too large'. No graphic record of either of these observations seems to have

survived, and certainly neither is shown on the plan in the 1928 edition of *The Roman Fort at Ribchester*.

The third edition of the Hopkinson report also recorded the excavation in 1927 of the fort's external bath-house. Several of the early travellers described a very large drain, which Stukeley said was large enough to stand up in. Whether or not this was the bath-house drain, the bath-house itself was apparently first discovered in 1837, when the tenant of the land, Mr Patchett, set out to make a hot-bed. 'He was surprised', said the *Preston Pilot*, 'to discover a spacious Roman Bath, being ten yards in length and five yards in breadth, and depth four feet. The bottom of the bath was covered with flags, which, with the sides, were covered with a thick coating of cement. On breaking it up, upwards of forty cartloads of stones were taken away from the place'. The description is slightly tantalising, both because of what it does say and because of what it does not mention. The size is perfectly adequate for a room in a bath-house, and the cement coating is also appropriate, but this does not usually cover the flagged floor, and neither *pilae* nor any kind of tile is mentioned. It is possible that the excavators found the upper part of the bath-house still standing four feet high, and that the cement-covered flagged floor was that of a heated room. It seems slightly improbable that they would not have broken through the floor at any point and so revealed the void beneath.

Also found at the same time was 'a leaden trough or cistern, about a foot wide and a yard long, and weighing nearly seventy pounds'. It seems likely that this was a fairly deep vessel. From the given dimensions and weight it can be calculated that if the vessel had been, say, 18 inches deep, it would have been made of lead weighing nearly five pounds per square foot. Since the heaviest of the three grades of modern plumbers' lead, normally used for roofing, was 'four-pound lead', it seems improbable that the vessel was much shallower than this, and therefore of thicker lead. This object may hint at some kind of industrial activity requiring the boiling of water. It is worth noting that lead pans used in the Cheshire salt industry in Roman times were considerably larger and shallower than the Ribchester pan seems to have been.

Whatever was found in 1837, there seems no doubt that the excavations of 1927 were close to the site of the 1837 find. They took place in Dr Patchett's orchard and revealed a large part of a bath-house of a type known from other cavalry forts. It had both monolithic stone *pilae* and others built up of square tiles. The two types of *pilae*, when taken together with the two furnaces found, clearly inserted in secondary positions within the building, suggests a two-period or two-phase

Figure 16. Part of the bath-house as excavated in 1927, showing both stone and tile *pilae*.

building. The general plan of the bath-house, with its circular *laconicum*, recalls that of Red House, Corbridge and others.

No more major work seems to have taken place before the Second World War, but one piece of what would now be called 'rescue archaeology' took place in 1938. Prior to the building of the house called Anchorholme in that year, an excavation was carried out by Donald Atkinson. No report was published, but in a letter to the Ministry of Works he reported 'the stuff is bad to dig' but that the evidence seemed to him to suggest 'wooden buildings occupied from *c*. A.D. 80 to the latter part of the second century, and then a levelling up of the whole area and the laying down of a gravel paving ... I think it is clear that only the administrative buildings remained after the Severan reconstruction and that the rest was parade ground'. It is not clear, if this was the case, who was to be the subject of the administration in the administrative buildings and who to parade on the parade ground.

After the Second World War, it was felt that a publication was needed to succeed the three editions of Hopkinson's pamphlet. The National Trust, which had been involved at the site since the early days of the Museum (see Chapter 7), brought in Professor Ian Richmond. As archaeological advisor to the Trust, he both supervised the consolidation of the granary ends and provided a new guide book. That *Guide* was exhausted by 1971, and the present author's *Guide* was then written. This has been adopted by the Museum Trust (as successors to the National Trust), and a second edition is planned.

The post-war excavations on the site have been limited by the availability of space and resources. Only four of them have been on any large scale. The earliest excavations seem to have been those conducted by Mr J. V. H. Eames of Liverpool University in 1953–1955. These were intended as training excavations, and their results were never published in detail. Some of the original

drawings and finds survive, however, together with duplicated reports for 1953 and 1954. Eames dug across the 'western' (i.e. south-western) defences. Here, in the field beyond the churchyard, is a substantial linear depression which has always been regarded as the remains of a Roman defensive ditch, presumably a late one, superseding earlier, probably multiple, version(s). We have seen that the existence of this ditch was known to all the early travellers and that their explanations for it formed a considerable part of their ideas about the site. Eames's 1953 excavations, however, convinced him that the depression was of natural origin, and it is true that, had a single wide and deep ditch been dug in late Roman times, it would presumably have obliterated the ditches whose remains were seen in excavations elsewhere in both 1970 and 1978.

Eames's other work was in the Rectory garden, and here he revealed a stratigraphic sequence which was not to be matched until 1990. Below five feet of rampart clay relating to the 'known' fort, he found the evidence of two very large and deep post-holes with the remains of the posts themselves surviving. These had been preceded by wattle and daub buildings. He felt that the posts were too close together to have been part of a gate tower or interval tower; however, he found the other posts in 1955, and, with the others, they formed a square. His note in the *Journal of Roman Studies* for 1956, however, described these features from top to bottom, ending 'Period 3 could be Flavian', in a manner which suggested that he was referring to the uppermost and latest of the three periods. It seemed likely afterwards that this represented an inversion, and that it was period 3, *counting from the top*, which was Flavian. The evidence of the Lancaster University Archaeological Unit's work in the churchyard extension in 1989–1990, however, seems to suggest that the report indeed meant exactly what it said.

After the very small scale excavations of 1953–1955 (the budget for 1953 was £50, with

Figure 17. Part of the bath-house as re-excavated in 1964. Most of what was seen in 1927 had survived, only to suffer from subsequent neglect.

a recommendation for an increase to £100 in 1954) no professionally-supervised excavation took place in Ribchester for fifteen years. That is not to say that the ground remained undisturbed. Within the village a number of small scale excavations took place which demonstrated the wide extent of the *vicus* in the late first and second centuries, and also produced little evidence for its existence in the third, and, particularly, the fourth, centuries. Potentially the most interesting, and sadly the least revealing, was a re-excavation of the bath-house in 1964. This exposed most of what had been seen in 1927 and, in some areas, more. Had it been possible to consolidate the remains, a splendid visitor attraction might have resulted. In the event, the site was allowed to remain open, and deteriorated steadily over the next dozen years. No more information was ultimately gained as a result of this excavation than was known in 1927. Conversely, much was lost in the way of loose *pilae*, tiles and so forth. What was produced was a puzzle for the subsequent excavators, who had to sort out the resulting jungle and add it to their results without the benefit of a report to refer to.

At much the same time that this was proceeding, other, more responsible, though under-resourced, excavations were taking place. Between 1965 and 1967 a site at the corner of Water Street and Damside Street was examined. This produced clear evidence of a building of more than one phase, together with much pottery and other material. The site itself was insufficiently large to enable a plan to be recovered, and despite suggestions that the building might have been a *mansio*, it has to be said that its chief importance lies in the evidence it gave for a very large and widely spreading *vicus*.

While the excavation of this site was in its latest stages, a small excavation took place at Anchor Hill. This name, it will be recalled, bulked large in the early accounts of the fort, and indeed the tail it represented very much wagged the dog. In fact, it is highly probable that all the alleged anchors, 'ship's rings', and even Pennant's unexaminable ship, were the result of self-fulfilling prophecies. T. D. Whitaker did not ultimately believe in the Roman port theory, as we have seen, and his suggestion to account for the alleged nautical *impedimenta* was that they represented no more than a ferry across the river. It seems more likely, however, that the explanation of the name lies in Anchor Hill's position close to the churchyard. Whitaker himself recorded the presence at Ribchester in the fourteenth century of an anchoress, or female hermit. Such mendicant recluses were commonplace in medieval times, and were frequently domiciled near the entrance to a churchyard, where charitable gifts from the people could be readily attracted and received. The analogy between the anchor of

a ship (deriving ultimately from a Greek word meaning a hook) and anchoress/anchorite (from another Greek word meaning to retire) had already struck the compiler of the medieval *vade mecum* for such people, the *Ancrene Riwle*: 'She is anchored under the church as an anchor under a ship so that neither waves nor storms may overwhelm it'. The archaeological importance of the 1967 Anchor Hill excavations lay in the fact that the pottery found included a few fourth century pieces.

The following year saw two small but interesting pieces of work. In one case members of Chorley Teachers' Training College excavated in the yard of the Clarendon Haulage Company. The excavation proved something of a disappointment, though it demonstrated the wide presence of waterlogged deposits at low levels in Ribchester. It did not, however, as hoped, add to the information provided by four burials in *amphorae* which had been seen earlier in the vicinity.

The other small excavation took place in the village playing field in 1968, and was designed merely to demonstrate the presence or absence of Roman levels there. Their clear recognition led directly to the next large scale excavation at Ribchester. This marked the beginning of the association of the late Professor G. D. B. Jones of Manchester University with the fort. The 1969 excavation was innovative and would not be done in the same way today. Its departure from received method lay in the use of mechanical equipment. Today the removal of topsoil and other sterile overburden by machinery is a standard procedure. In 1969 it was decided to make use of the new power and precision of earth-moving machinery to cut long sample trenches through the playing field. These, when their sections and floors were cleaned up, yielded a surprising amount of information about the *vicus*.

The chief structures encountered and recognised were timber buildings and clay furnaces. The timber buildings, parts of some twenty of which were noted, were of post and wattle construction, and in one case part of a wattle partition which had fallen was excavated. Timber work of a more substantial kind, including pegged mortice-and-tenon joints, was also recovered. All timber was excellently preserved in water-logged deposits. The furnaces appeared as brown clay dumps with their central portions turned red by fire. Nevertheless, they seemed to have been used in a fairly low temperature process, and one yielded an unburnt coin of Trajan from its filling. It would, of course, be of great interest to be able to recover the plan of one or more of these *vicus* buildings, and it is probable that, were that ever to become possible, the 1969 trenches would be found not to have greatly damaged them.

At the end of the second century, much of the area had been sealed by a deep deposit of gravel, and the temptation was widely felt in 1969 to identify this as a parade ground imposed by military *diktat*, and resulting from the needs of the Sarmatian garrison apparently stationed at Ribchester in or about A.D. 175. It is interesting in this connection to digress for a moment to remember that, although the sending of 5,500 Sarmatians to Britain by Marcus Aurelius is recorded by Cassius Dio, there is no proof, as Dr David Breeze has pointed out, that these were the only, or the earliest, Sarmatians to be sent to Britain. Indeed, it was suggested in 1928 that the Sarmatians whose inscriptions are known from Ribchester had been recruited during Trajan's Dacian wars nearly a century earlier than those of Marcus Aurelius.

The 1969 excavation had been a 'research' excavation prompted only by a desire to know more. It was immediately followed in 1970 by a 'rescue' excavation. This dichotomy is much disliked by some, and is more real in some cases than others. At Ribchester in 1970 the projected line of an intended road produced a threat to Roman levels, which in turn resulted in the provision of government (Department of the Environment) funds.

Nevertheless, had resources been offered for excavation in Ribchester 'without strings', the area threatened would have been high on the list of priorities for 'research' reasons.

The road concerned was to be built as a consequence of an improvement to the village's sewerage system. The existing sewage plant lay on the opposite side of Boyce's Brook to the Roman bath-house. Since Boyce's Brook discharges into the Ribble upstream of the village, this was considered undesirable, and a new plant was proposed downstream. The plan was for lorries servicing the plant to drive through the village to the bottom of Church Street, along the river bank in front of the Rectory and then to pass between Anchorholme and Churchgates along a new piece of road behind Lower Alston Farm. Thus, part of the *retentura* of the fort and part of the 'western' defences were under threat. The resulting excavations were the first, and so far the only ones, to demonstrate the existence within the fort of timber barrack blocks and possible stables. We can only be glad, as we look at the state of traffic in the village today, and the recent necessity to strengthen the river bank in front of the Rectory, that wisdom prevailed and the new road was ultimately constructed to pass north and west of the fort area rather than through it.

Among small scale works at about this time was an attempt to locate the *via quintana* of the fort in the garden of Churchgates, and, in 1971, observations were made on a building site in Greenside. Here, the remains of substantial timber posts set in clay were seen in foundation trenches. Again they do little more than demonstrate the extent of the *vicus*, but this can, by such means, be shown to underlie most of the present village, and therefore to be of a comparable size to such well-known examples as Old Carlisle.

In 1972 further work was done on the Water Street site, but the increasing popularity of Ribchester, both with visitors and as a place of residence, was to prompt two more pieces of rescue archaeology in the next two years. The first of these came with the construction of a substantial car park for the village. Here, four small trenches recovered the line of a road heading north-westwards, presumably that leaving the north-west gate of the fort. Evidence for ribbon development along it was found, but occupation was not thought to spread far from it. The 1974 excavation lay to the south of the known site of the bath-house, and was designed to test the archaeological potential of the area, in advance of the building of a house. In the event the house proposal was withdrawn and the small trenches dug showed that Roman archaeology lay very close to the surface here.

Not long after this, the sewerage scheme, for which the road had been proposed in 1970, was installed. It involved the laying of sewers along the village streets and north of the playing field to connect with the new sewage plant. The archaeological unit at Lancaster University, in conjunction with numerous helpers, watched the digging of the trenches, carried out two small excavations and recorded much information. The scheme resulted in the discovery of at least two wells, one containing part of a barrel, and finds were made throughout the village, though little systematic information could be obtained from the contractor's trenches.

Almost at the same time as the sewerage works were being completed a rear access road was built behind the houses in Water Street, running from Greenside towards the site of the Roman bath-house. The excavations in advance of the construction of this road showed that the bath-house itself did not extend into this area, and that beside one small foundation, there was not much evidence of the *vicus* either. Although the extent of the *vicus* is clearly considerable, there were also, as one might expect, gaps in the buildings, just as there are in the present-day village. While the access road excavations were in progress, an extension was being added to the village school, and the excavation

team was able to keep an eye on the foundation trenches. These yielded considerable signs of timber buildings and one or two finds of interest in themselves, such as a wooden spindle; spindle-whorls in all sorts of inorganic materials are frequent finds, but the organic (wood or bone) spindle itself is seldom seen. Another find was a large part of a shale dish. Roman exploitation of shale deposits at such well known sites as Kimmeridge (Dorset) is well documented. Most artefacts made from this soft, easily shaped rock are turned on a lathe, and comprise such things as dishes and bracelets. Indeed, shale bracelets are known from Ribchester. The dish from the foundation trench of the school, however, was unusual in that it was ovoid in shape, and must therefore have been carved by hand. It is not unlike one found many years ago in a Roman *villa* at Rew Street on the Isle of Wight (*Ant. Jnl.* 26 (1936) 202–203).

The following year saw an excavation which marked a change in excavation administration and pointed a lesson which it now seems odd that it was necessary to learn. Funding was obtained for the excavation of the bath-house. This meant a combined operation mingling a clearance and planning of the mess left after the 1964 'excavation' with the excavation proper of most of the rest of the site. This was to be done under the auspices of the Lancashire County Museum Service, with the aim of leaving a consolidated visitor attraction at the end. This was all largely achieved, although the vulnerability of exposed tile floors to frost meant that they had to be replaced with gravel. What was not realised, however, was the extent to which most excavations relied on good will and spare time work by academics. In this case a director was employed without the inclusion in his contract of time and resources for post-excavation work, writing up and publishing. This is elementary today; and while many deplore the 'commercialisation' of excavation, such a system goes a long way to ensuring that such work does get

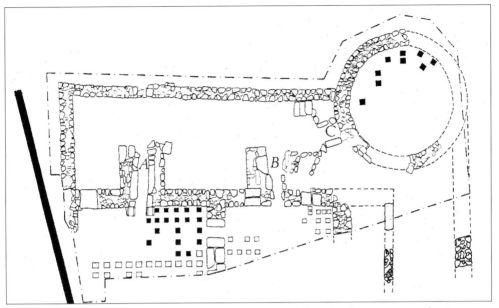

Figure 18. Composite plan of part of the bath-house, incorporating information from 1927, 1964 and 1978.

done. Examples of the old method where neither post-excavation specialist work nor publishing get done are not hard to find.

The last part of the sewerage scheme took place in 1978, when a pipe was run from the Rectory through the southern corner of the fort and across the south-western defences. The results of the archaeological examination of this largely confirmed the observations from the 1970 excavations, though there were anomalies.

In 1980, two threats to the archaeology of the village were pre-empted by excavation. The more obvious of these came from the proposal to build sheltered housing to the west of the car park, and only just across a road from areas of known Roman archaeology revealed by the sewerage scheme. The 1980 excavation resulted in the identification of a rampart and ditch system which seems to have been a defended boundary of the vicus, interesting information indeed, for few such settlements are known to have had defences. The same excavation revealed, entirely unexpectedly, an arc of five Bronze

Age cremations in urns. This was an intriguing footnote to the story of settlement in the village, but additionally interesting in that few such burial sites are known from lowland sites, though there are one or two others in the Ribble valley.

The other threat was less obvious, and its recognition as a bona fide threat requiring response took some diligent argument. It had long been recognised that the digging of graves in the churchyard was liable to produce Roman artefacts, and successive sextons had co-operated in reporting such finds. One of Eames's objectives in 1954 had been to check that the area next to be used for burial was sterile. What was done in 1980 was to excavate a long section north-south across the churchyard extension. This produced evidence of a rampart and ditch system of some complexity which was entirely unexpected.

Two further pieces of work by the then Cumbria and Lancashire Archaeological Unit, now the University of Lancaster Archaeological Unit, take the story into the last decade of the twentieth century. From 1989–1991 the

Figure 19. Two photographs of the visit of the Time Team in 1992. In the first Mick Aston (centre) talks to Phil Harding, while Tony Robinson trowels. In the second, the arrangements of a mobile, rail-mounted camera can be seen.

logical follow up of the 1980 churchyard extension dig took place. This took the form of an area excavation at the eastern end of the ground designated for future burials, and its results reinforced and added to those of 1980, the chief addition being the discovery of the rampart to which the ditch system which had been seen in 1980 belonged. The rampart was laid on timber strapping and within its structure were also found the four posts of what was presumably an interval tower. This rampart and its associated features have very important implications for the history of the fort, as will be seen in a later chapter. Information about later activity in the area excavated was also of great interest, but was of a less revolutionary nature.

Throughout the site, the degree of preservation of all organic materials was exceptionally good, and much new information is resulting as this is worked through. This fact, and the necessity for detailed information on the defences and buildings found, emphasise that there is never a right time to write such an account as this. New ideas and information are always in the pipeline, and are liable to overtake the work of any author, especially if he is trying to produce an overall picture.

This is further underlined by the second of the pieces of work referred to above. Casual finds have always shown that the extent of the Roman occupation at Ribchester was unusually great. Finds of Roman material have been made from time to time right out to the edges of the modern village. Plans to build housing, in 1991, on the site of one of Ribchester's two nineteenth century textile mills, demolished a little earlier, were therefore the occasion of further work by LUAU. It was thought unlikely that anything of significance would appear, but in the event traces of linear features and of buildings showed that Roman occupation had occurred there, and a number of theories have been advanced to account for its presence. One or more of the possible theories may ultimately be ruled out by detailed study of dating evidence from the site.

What is worth considering about all the work described is this: evidence for the Roman occupation of Ribchester is a finite resource. What survives in the ground can only diminish, and it behoves us to treat it accordingly. The greater part of the fort site and the area of occupation surrounding it is either lost to river erosion or sealed by modern occupation. Most of the very small remainder is protected by legislation. The days of the shoe-string excavation are over. It may be a little sad that some of the fun of early amateur excavations, or excavations only lightly supervised by professionals, has gone, but in terms of proportion of available evidence recovered, and thereby rendered usable, the modern excavation is greatly superior, and it is right that it should prevail.

Some idea of the change which has taken place is shown by a comparison of Eames's £50 budget of 1953 as against the Unit's expenditure on the churchyard extension, and post-excavation work on its resultant material, of perhaps £300,000. Even today no inflation factor can explain that. All sorts of explanations can be given for parts of the difference, such as the payment of workers as opposed to the use of volunteers; but in the end it must be said that what the money does is to enable something much closer to the maximum amount of available information to be extracted from the evidence. It should

not occur, as it has in the past, that degradable materials are excavated, not examined at the time for fear of damage, stored against the day when conservation resources were available, and simply disintegrate because no such day has ever dawned.

We have followed in some detail the way in which our knowledge of the Roman occupation of Ribchester has been gained. We have seen how that knowledge has moved from a state of semi-superstitious awe to the modern demystified scientific explanation. Chapters 5 and 6 will attempt to draw together the threads of some four centuries of study to produce a late twentieth-century 'snapshot' of Roman Ribchester. It is a picture in which parts will be out of focus. Some of these will come into focus as time and further work progress. Some will ultimately be seen to be quite different from how they appear today. But this is is the fascination of archaeology. Research is always advancing knowledge, and the picture will never be quite perfect.

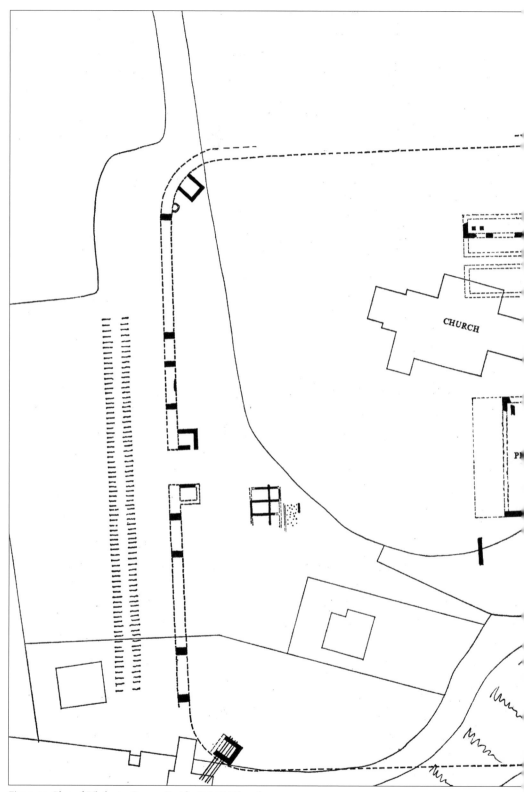

Figure 20. Plan of Ribchester Roman Fort by B. J. N. Edwards.

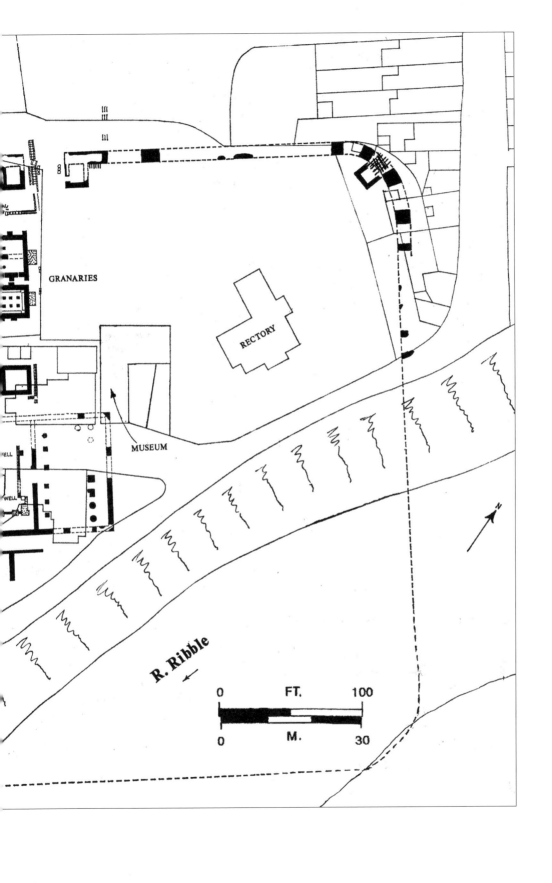

GRANARIES

RECTORY

MUSEUM

WELL

WELL

R. Ribble

0   FT.   100

0   M.   30

CHAPTER FIVE

The Fort in the First and Second Centuries A.D.

A few years ago, this would have been the easiest part of the story of Roman Ribchester to write. As long ago as 1800 T. D. Whitaker had decided, on the basis solely of his reading of Classical authorities, that the fort at Ribchester had been established under the governorship of Agricola (A.D. 77–83) When the evidence of archaeology began to be added to Whitaker's assessment of Classical authors, in the twentieth century, there appeared to be no reason to change the attribution. The earliest coinage and pottery from the site dated from the last decades of the first century, and there was nothing in the dating methods available which was sophisticated enough to determine more precisely when the fort was established. Documentary history and archaeology appeared to be marching in satisfactory harmony.

At the same time, received wisdom was that, although during the governorship of Petillius Cerialis (A.D. 71–74) forts further north than Ribchester had been established, Cerialis's route had been from the neighbourhood of York *via* Stainmore to the vicinity of Penrith. This had always been a somewhat strange idea, since it left a substantial area of north-west England isolated and by-passed, only for that area to be incorporated in the Empire a few years later, in Agricola's campaigns. Even this process left the Lake District by-passed; but this seemed less improbable in that the nature of the terrain was difficult, and the idea of by-passing that area and coming back to finish the job could be seen as analogous to the treatment of north Wales somewhat earlier.

Various factors have undermined this picture and required its reconsideration. For example, the incidence of Flavian coinage found around the lower reaches of the Ribble and the Mersey suggested earlier use of these estuaries than would have been the case had they been among the estuaries referred to by Tacitus in his account of the campaign of the second year of Agricola's governorship.

More recently, the dating by dendrochronology of timbers in the earliest Roman levels at Carlisle to A.D. 71–73 has firmly supported the idea of Roman penetration at least as far as that under Cerialis. The question of whether or not this related to an advance *via* Stainmore looked difficult to answer. No fort in north-west England seemed particularly likely to resolve the dilemma by producing the required closely-dated evidence. As a result, those who felt that Cerialis rather than Agricola might have been the first Roman governor to incorporate what is now north-west England within the Empire were forced to suggest that the apparent absence of evidence for the former's activities was due to the fact that Cerialis was 'not a builder of forts'.

Some, at least, of the mental confusion about the earlier phases of the Roman occupation of north-west England is produced by the various adjectives used in its discussion. Thus, 'Agricolan' means during the governorship of Gn. Julius Agricola and 'Cerialian' during that of Q. Petillius Cerialis. Coin finds which might relate to these periods or earlier ones are usually referred to by the name of the Emperor issuing the coins, while dynastic

Figure 21. Gold *aureus* of Vespasian
(Emperor A.D. 69–79).

Figure 22. Gold *aureus* of Domitian
(Emperor A.D. 81–96).

adjectives such as 'Flavian' are also used. The usefulness of these adjectives is, of course, that they are somewhat less precise than actual dates. Coin issues may well be precisely dateable, but the activity to which they relate did not necessarily occur in the year of their issue. Historical events such as the appointment and recall of governors may also be dateable, though not always unequivocally.

It is now beginning to look certain that the earliest Roman penetration of north-west England was Cerialian or earlier, in terms of governorships; that it involved combined operations by land and sea; and that it left little in the way of discoverable archaeological traces, though the site at Kirkham may be an exception. It also seems likely that the advance under Cerialis as governor towards Carlisle was achieved by the IXth legion, based at Lincoln. Cerialis had once been its legate (Commanding Officer), while Agricola, later to follow Cerialis as governor (though not directly) was, during Cerialis's governorship, legate of the XXth legion, based at Wroxeter and likely to have operated on the west side of the country.

Like many another negative, the idea that Cerialis, as governor, was not a builder

of forts, is difficult to prove, but it did look as though the problem might have been cracked when the 1989 excavations at Ribchester produced an early rampart laid on timber 'corduroy'. All that was necessary was for a few timbers to show evidence of having been felled in the 70s A.D. Sadly, of the timbers submitted for dendrochronological dating, none was certainly datable as a result of a lack of surviving sapwood. This does not mean that such timbers do not exist, or that the rampart base is not as early as has been suggested – only that the required evidence has not been produced. Nevertheless, the excavators were confident that the earliest phase of activity dated from the governorship of Cerialis and that the second phase represented the re-use of the fort during Agricola's campaigns as governor.

What, then, of this early fort? Its discovery produced something of a shock for received opinion about the development of Roman Ribchester. Previously, the development had been seen as beginning with a fort enclosed by turf and clay ramparts based on timber 'corduroy', and presumably carrying timber defences. The buildings within that fort were also assumed to have been of timber, and indeed the only structures so far excavated from elsewhere than the central range (just outside the churchyard wall in 1970) were of this material. No attempt was made, when either the *principia* or the granaries were excavated at the beginning of the twentieth century, to probe beneath them for possible timber predecessors. Subsequent modifications had always been treated as though the size of the fort remained constant from its presumed Agricolan beginnings.

Hints did exist that the situation might be different. For example, Eames, in 1953, had seen evidence for a four-post structure with very large timbers which now looks as though it might have been another in the series with the timber tower discovered in the churchyard extension in 1989. Again, in 1970, although the trenches were relatively restricted, and the alignment of the earliest buildings found appeared to be the same as that of later buildings, the former were somewhat different in nature from the later ones, for which a very good case was made out for identification as barracks. The churchyard extension ramparts were certainly on a slightly different alignment from that of the previously known forts at Ribchester, and the suggestions were made that they represented the defences of the earliest Roman establishment there, and that their scale meant that they might derive from something rather larger than a conventional fort – a fort which might have been sufficient for a legionary vexillation perhaps brigaded with auxiliaries. Most of that is speculation, and depends on the discovery and examination of further elements in the earliest fort. It is clear, however, that the earliest known fort, apart from that discovered in the churchyard extension, was of timber and turf with timber buildings, elsewhere than in the central range. Those buildings were all excavated in the early days of scientific excavation, and were afterwards either concealed by building or consolidated and left exposed. No real attempt seems to have been made to penetrate deep enough

to check whether or not they had timber predecessors.

Two tantalising little pieces of evidence relating to Ribchester at this time have been found among the ink writing tablets discovered at *Vindolanda*, in Northumberland. One of these, from a man called Oppius Niger, was written to one Crispinus at *Vindolanda*. It seems likely that each was the garrison commander at his respective posting, and that Niger is reporting that he has sent further on their way from *Bremetennacum* men from Crispinus' First Cohort of Tungrians, who were taking something to the Governor of the province. If that is the correct interpretation, it suggests that the Governor was then at Chester, or at least not at York, the route to which from *Vindolanda* would not pass through Ribchester.

The other letter is from two men, Niger and Brocchus, and was written to Flavius Cerialis, who seems likely to have been another commander at *Vindolanda*. It is not certain that the Niger of this letter is the same man at that of the letter to Crispinus, but it seems likely on palaeographical grounds. Cerialis was apparently likely soon to meet the provincial Governor, perhaps also while he was at Chester.

There is even a hint, in the letters 'brem', perhaps the beginning of *Bremetennacum*, that Ribchester may also have been mentioned on one of the ink writing tablets found at Carlisle. These tablets from *Vindolanda* and Carlisle, written in ink on thin slivers of wood, preserve details of both official documents and unofficial correspondence, and are among the most exciting recent discoveries to shed entirely new lights on Roman Britain. The waterlogged conditions so frequently found at Ribchester should preserve such things, and it is a fascinating thought that future excavations might uncover some, particularly now that the possibility of their presence and their appearance is recognised.

The fort also possessed, apparently from an early stage, both a bath-house and a *vicus*, or civilian settlement. The former of these was of a type most commonly known from cavalry forts, though there is no obvious reason why the nature of the unit in garrison should be related to the design of the bathhouse. As for the garrison, this has always been said to have been *ala II Asturum*, a cavalry unit of 500 men, as were all cavalry units in Roman Britain with the exception of *ala Petriana*, a unit of 1000 men stationed, for most of the period from the early second century, at Stanwix, just outside Carlisle. There was more than one *ala Asturum*, and the Ribchester unit is usually quoted as *ala II Asturum* on the basis of the inscription on the altar RIB 586. The figure II on this, however, is not recorded by Camden, who saw the altar, and depends on a nineteenth-century reading which omits the letters DEC(urio), which Camden *did* record. In fact, the assignment of *ala II Asturum* as the garrison at Ribchester in what remained of the first century after the fort's foundation and the second century up to A.D. 175 depends on the following rather unsatisfactory sequence: given that an *ala Asturum* was at Ribchester (RIB 586), it cannot have been *ala I Asturum* in the first and early second centuries, because we know that unit was elsewhere; Ribchester cannot have had an *ala Asturum* in garrison at any other time because after 175 it was garrisoned by the Sarmatians, 7,500 of whom were levied, Cassius Dio tells us, by Marcus Aurelius and sent to Britain in that year. RIB 594 and 595 refer to *ala Sarmatarum*, and are undated but probably third century; RIB 583 and 587, between them covering most of the years from A.D. 222–244, call the unit *numerus equitum Sarmatarum Bremetennacensium*; and the *Notitia Dignitatum*, a late Roman army list, assigns Ribchester the *cuneus Sarmatarum*. The titles *numerus* and *cuneus* are not those of regular Roman auxiliary troops, and suggest a recognition of the situation which would doubtless arise by A.D. 200, when veterans of *ala Sarmatarum* were discharged and

Figure 23. Cavalry tombstone found in the river, 1876.

returned to their native places, had those still been within the Empire. That they were not presumably accounts for the title *veteranorum* added to Ribchester's name about that time, implying, as it does, that Sarmatian veterans were settled in the surrounding area.

It was also in about the last quarter of the second century that much of the *vicus* to the north-west of the fort came to the end of its life and the area was sealed with a heavy gravel layer. This has been plausibly explained as a parade ground for the newly-arrived Sarmatians, though it is not clear why they should have needed different parade arrangements from the garrison who preceded them,

Asturian or otherwise. Parade grounds are not as readily accepted today as once they were, but alternative reasons for the obliteration of the *vicus* at the end of the second century have not been forthcoming.

The date of the conversion of the turf and timber defences of the fort into stone ones has not been demonstrated conclusively at Ribchester. It is assumed, on the basis of many analogous cases, to have been in the reign of Hadrian. There is, however, a danger that the number of similar cases known include some with as little direct evidence as Ribchester, and that a circular argument results. There is at least a possibility that the conversion took place as late as the middle of the second century, when troops of the Sixth legion are recorded as having worked there. It is also true that the coin evidence from the site as a whole suggests a slight hiatus in the first half of the century. Taken together, all these pieces of evidence might well represent a temporary withdrawal of, or reduction in, the garrison at the time of the construction of Hadrian's Wall, and a return to full strength in the Antonine period, possibly after the abandonment of the Antonine Wall itself.

CHAPTER SIX

The Fort in the Third and Fourth Centuries A.D.

If we assume that the third century opened for Ribchester with the normal date for the discharge of veterans from the *ala Sarmatarum*, it must also have opened with something of a crisis for the fort commander. What was he to do with these veterans? We have aleady seen that return to their homeland was not an available option, and the crisis was made more acute by the fact that probably most of the veterans due for discharge had actually come from beyond the Danube. It is fairly clear that, although Roman auxiliary units often had titles of geographical origin based on the area in which they were originally raised, in the same way that infantry units in the British army had, and to some extent still have, those Roman units frequently stayed in garrison at one place for such long periods that local recruiting must have been the norm. This must have happened particularly in the case of the Sarmatians, because any deficiency in their numbers caused by disease or military action could not have been supplied by recruitment from their area of origin, since it had passed out of the Empire.

There is, of course, no sure knowledge of the answer to the commanding officer's dilemma. We have no historical record of its occurrence, still less of its solution. What we do have, however, is evidence that the fort became known as *Bremetennacum veteranorum*, and that at least one of its commanders had the additional title of *centurio regionarius*. This has been interpreted to mean that the Sarmatian veterans were settled in the area surrounding Ribchester, and that the commanding officer of the fort was given the additional task of controlling them. In a characteristic piece of insight, Sir Ian Richmond suggested that the veterans might have been engaged in breeding the heavy horses needed by their compatriots and successors, and that the Fylde of Lancashire would have been an ideal area in which to do this. Unfortunately, no evidence has emerged to support this idea in the half century since it was propounded, but it remains an attractive scenario. The *centurio regionarius*, however, is a less weighty piece of support than might be thought. The title has parallels, without the special circumstances existing at Ribchester about A.D. 200, and it is clear from the evidence of papyri that Roman troops in Egypt, at least, performed many non-military duties within what was referred to as their

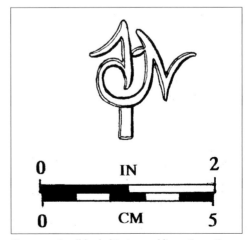

Figure 24. Small lead object resembling a Sarmatian 'tamga' sign.

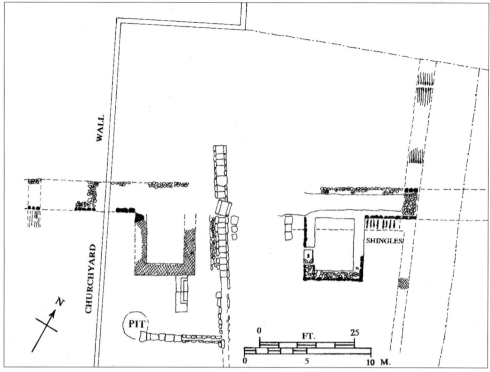

Figure 25. Thomas May's plan of the north gate.

regio. At neither Manchester nor Carlisle, at both of which places in north-west England a *centurio regionarius* is thought to have existed, are the circumstances known to have been particularly unusual at the time.

We must presume that the Sarmatian unit, whatever its precise title and whatever its source of recruits, remained Ribchester's garrison well into the fourth century, and probably until the end of the existence of the fort as such. Certainly we have no record of any other unit at the time, though it is always possible that this state of affairs is the result of accident – by no means all units known to have been in garrison at Roman forts have left tangible evidence of their presence. However, there is a very good representation of the third century among the recorded inscriptions from the site. We have a building inscription possibly of A.D. 208, an altar of

A.D. 216–219, a temple dedication of A.D. 222–235 and part of a dedicatory monument of A.D. 238–244 or later. The fort with its nominally Sarmatian garrison was certainly the scene of much activity in the third century, however much or little of that activity was due to the garrison itself.

There seems to be no doubt, either, that the fort was occupied during a large part of the fourth century. The evidence of pottery alone would assure us of this. The coin evidence is slightly less clear, and indeed the sequence ends, rather surprisingly, with a *solidus* of the Emperor Gratian. This coin was issued in A.D. 373, though, of course, it may have come to Ribchester some time later. That there was later activity there is shown by the amount of late-fourth century pottery, and particularly of calcite-gritted (Crambeck) ware dating to later than A.D. 367. Further, although the *vicus* seems to have come to a fairly abrupt end in the latter part of the second century, that does not appear to have been the fate of the bath-house. As one might expect, this seems to have continued in use, and the only fourth century coins recorded from outside the fort come from its vicinity.

As to the actual end of the life of the Roman fort we have no evidence. The nature of the site, with so much of the actual fort area built over, precludes the possibility of the large area excavations which have yielded such fascinating evidence about what is often called 'sub-Roman' life at such sites as Wroxeter or Birdoswald. We can say, of course, with complete confidence that there was never a day when 'the Romans left'. By the time we are discussing, everyone was a Roman, and their 'departure' would have been an impossibility. There is no doubt, in general terms, that military forces were reduced as a result of the activities of the various adventurers and claimants to the Empire in the later fourth century. Equally, though less obviously, the infrastructure which supported the soldiers was undermined. Ultimately, the end of Britain as a part of the Roman Empire must have come by administrative and financial means, rather than by fire and sword. The inhabitants of one particular corner of the Ribble valley must have been aware, on a particular date in the latter part of the first century, that Roman power had arrived there; they would not, of course, have had any idea of how long-lasting that state of affairs was to be. But their late-fourth or early-fifth century successors would not have been aware until some time after the event that over three hundred years of being part of a great political entity had come to an end.

If we know little of how and when that process took place, we know even less of the state of affairs which replaced it. There can be no doubt that life went on, without many of the more desirable elements which people had come to take for granted. For the soldiers,

Figure 26. Gold *solidus* of Gratian (Emperor A.D. 367–383). The latest coin from the site.

both pay and orders ceased to arrive, as did supplies of all kinds. For other local inhabitants, both their protection and their most important market largely disappeared. The last of the soldiers must have been forced to acquire many of the necessities of life by their own efforts and without the benefit of a money economy. The local people probably continued to some extent to facilitate this, but they, too, must have had to adapt to a non-money economy. If it is difficult for us to visualise life in the fort at the height of the Roman civilisation, it is much more difficult to envisage its gradual end. Sadly, we cannot recognise archaeologically the evidence for the processes we have been considering. Since people must have used artefacts and produced varying effects on the environment, we ought to be able to do so. For the present, just as the inhabitants who preceded the arrival of Roman power are difficult to detect, so are those who followed its disappearance. Archaeologically, at least, there is something to be said for the point of view which leads us to label much of the first four centuries of our era 'the Roman interlude'.

CHAPTER SEVEN

The Museum

One of the features which most readily distinguishes Ribchester among modern villages sited on or near Roman forts is the presence there of a museum. The museum represents a continuing monument to local initiative, and is no small factor in the interest shown in the village by large numbers of visitors.

According to a report drawn up in 1911, almost certainly by D. N. Haslewood of Robinson and Haslewood, Solicitors, of Blackburn, the idea of a museum at Ribchester was brought forward in 1908, and a first meeting was held to discuss the idea in September of that year. Since Thomas May was still excavating as late as May, 1908, it is highly probable that he was privy to the first glimmerings of the idea.

That the idea itself was Miss Greenall's there seems to be no doubt, and that she remained a moving spirit throughout the first few years is amply demonstrated. Six more meetings were held in 1909, 1910 and January, 1911, and by February, 1911, a leaflet for a public appeal was in proof. This summarised the situation at Ribchester, saying: 'During the last few years the Manchester and District Branch of the Classical Association has had in hand the excavation, previously begun by Professor Garstang, of Liverpool University, and Mr Thomas May, of Warrington, on the site of the Roman fort at Ribchester ... The foundations of part of the outer wall of the camp and of one of the four great gateways have been uncovered, and two large stone-built buildings which had apparently served as the granaries of the camp have been partially cleared'. It went on to state the desirability of keeping some of the excavated buildings open to view, of retaining finds on the site and of making them accessible to the public.

What this meant in practical terms is described thus:- 'For that purpose a strong local Committee was formed having originally Bishop Thornton, of Blackburn [Assistant Bishop of the Diocese of Manchester] as President, Miss Greenall, of Churchgates, Ribchester, as Honorary Secretary, and Mr T. H. Rymer, as Honorary Treasurer ... [which] has already arranged that the important parts of the excavated areas should be enclosed with railings ..., but has not yet been able to erect a museum owing to lack of funds ... The most important part of the site still unexcavated is occupied by an old ... building ... used as a Church Sunday School, and ... if this can be removed, and the ground excavated, many important problems connected with the central buildings of the Fort may be solved, and the volume on Roman Ribchester, which has for some years been in preparation ... can be ... published.' Having pointed out that the parish and archaeologists alike might gain their respective aims more cheaply if they acted together, the leaflet went on to recommend '(1) That the old Schoolroom be demolished and a new Parish room ... erected on an adjacent site; (2) That a Museum be erected immediately adjacent to the Parish room, but having a separate entrance; (3) That the site of the demolished Schoolroom be excavated under the auspices of the Classical Association ... [The] Museum building and site [would be conveyed] to the National Trust ... [and] would be controlled by a Committee of Management elected locally ...' The estimated costs of these operations were:- Parish Hall, £650;

Museum, £200; Excavation and Publication, £200. Of the total of £1050 thus estimated, £200 had already been raised.

It might be as well to explain here that the details of the early stages of the erection and operation of the museum can be reconstructed because one of the members of the committee was Col. J. W. R. Parker, C.B., F.S.A., of Browsholme Hall near Clitheroe, and he seems never to have thrown away a letter or telegram he received. These documents are among the voluminous family papers deposited at the Lancashire Record Office.

Having approved the form of the appeal leaflet, the Committee, by now under the Chairmanship of A. G. Rawstorne, first and only Bishop of Whalley, went on to consider ways of preventing more than one member sending an appeal to the same potential contributor. There does not appear to have been any consideration of more than one possible architect, and indeed the use of J. A. Seward, of Preston, Diocesan Surveyor for the Archdeaconries of Lancaster and Blackburn, may have been unavoidable for the Committee.

Seward's first proposal, submitted in October, 1911, was for a self-contained Museum separated from the Parish room by a party wall. The Parish room was to accommodate 300 people, there were to be a Class Room, a yard and, to the west of the building, an open space. Col. Parker suggested the provision of a lavatory and a gallery. The Committee seems to have thought the former a good idea, but Seward pointed out that the latter would increase the cost, at which the Committee suggested incorporating corbels for a possible later gallery if funds did not stretch to one immediately.

Hopes had been expressed at meetings in 1909 and 1910 that while the excavations of the old Schoolroom site would be under the auspices of the Classical Association, that body would also make a substantial contribution towards the cost of the Museum, and

the Association, in turn, had expressed a desire to be consulted on its design. In the event, the Classical Association appeared as the recipient of an expenditure item in the accounts, no income identifiably connected with the Association appearing. It did, however, approve the plan, and Hopkinson, on their behalf, asked for the provision of a back door to the Museum.

By the end of 1911 a crisis was looming. On the 11th of December Miss Greenall wrote to Col. Parker in some perplexity, unable to explain why Seward had apparently reduced the width of the passage (presumably that leading to the rear of the building) from 'a Cart way to 5 ft.' She quoted her brother as having foreseen difficulty in fitting in all that the Classical Association and the Rector required, and she was prepared, with Mr Sagar and Col. Parker, to dispense with the Museum lavatory. All was revealed to Col. Parker, probably in the same post, because he also received a letter from Seward, written on the same day as Miss Greenall's, explaining that he had been working from a plan, supplied to him and signed by the Rector, which gave the Parish Hall a frontage of 84 ft., with an additional 18 ft. for the Museum, whereas his own survey of the old building, made with a view to re-using its materials, had shown him that only 84 ft. in total was available.

Seward evidently found no great difficulty in amending the plans, and concern passed for a time to the necessity or otherwise of a back door to the Parish room. Miss Greenall pointed out the multifarious uses to which the Class Room would be put, including band practice, at the same time as such activities as sewing classes were occupying the main room. Lack of a back door would lead to 'much extra cleaning, to say nothing of the disagreeableness of the Bandsmen and others coming through the large room when we were working.'

By early January, 1912, amended plans were being sent and all seemed calm until, on January 25th, Miss Greenall sent a telegram to Col. Parker – 'Rector offered another and far better site anxious for your opinion for meeting could you come over today'. Whether or not the colonel was able to drop everything and come immediately, a meeting was held on 12th February which decided 'that the original site of the plans adopted on the 14th November 1911 be adhered to', and which received permission to encroach on the Rector's yard and shippon to carry out the plans.

By June, all seemed to be going well again until Seward dropped his bombshell. The buildings, as then planned, would cost £1600 – £600 for the Museum and £1000 for the Parish room. Col. Parker evidently cited the school at Waddington as a model, which prompted Miss Greenall , who had called the figure of £1600 'simply appalling', to write 'I know the school at Waddington and such a one would have been quite sufficient for Ribchester, had not the site been in such close proximity to the Church and Rectory, but even a plain building could soon have been made quite pretty with ivy and creepers'.

Summer then supervened, with important people away on holiday, and it was late August before a chat between the Bishop of Whalley and Seward led to the latter's offering to design a building at about £1200. The Bishop would clearly have preferred £1000. By late October, Seward had submitted another plan, and a letter from him to Col. Parker suggests that the latter had said that such a building should not cost more than £700. Seward said this was not possible, adding 'Ribchester is by no means a cheap place for building'. He had costed the building at 4d. per cu. ft., giving a price of £1033, and opined that this was the lowest rate possible.

In January, 1913, Mr Openshaw of Hothersall Hall joined the Committee, much to the satisfaction of both Miss Greenall and the Bishop. This resulted in a flurry of activity on the part of the Bishop, who visited Seward with Openshaw, informed him that 'the plans *must* be reduced to £1000', then visited

Openshaw taking Seward's latest ideas. In submitting Seward's £1000 plan, the Bishop noted that the main room was to be 54 ft. rather than 60 ft. in length, and slightly narrower; the roof was to be single span, without valley gutters, etc.; the materials 'plainer and less expensive'; the platform to be replaced with a movable version; and both Class Room and Museum to be slightly smaller. He ended with a suggestion that further economies could be made, e.g. 'the ceiling of the Museum appears to me *quite* unnecessary'.

There is a hint of friction in the observation that 'Mr Openshaw and I feel that if the Classical Association want to go forward before we agree to their doing so, we ought to require a certain proportion of the share represented by the cost of the Museum to be in hand'. There was about £380 in the account, but little of it was for the Museum.

Signs of impatience are evident by March, 1913, with Col. Parker evidently suggesting finding another architect, a move which the Bishop was rather against, but with the land paid for and conveyances drawn, there was clearly some straining at the leash in Ribchester. In calling a meeting in April, the Bishop pointed out that obtaining another tender would still leave the Committee in considerable debt to Seward for all the plans he had drawn, and he hinted, perhaps a little naughtily, that changing the plans might invalidate the conveyances of the land.

There had evidently been a little difficulty with these conveyances. Seward, as we have seen, had told Col. Parker in 1911 that the errors in measurement had been due to his using a plan which had been supplied to him. Shortly after this, Miss Greenall had written indignantly to Col. Parker: 'Mr Seward *did not* tell me that his measurements had been wrong and so I did not inderstand the delay until I had the Bishop's letter.' Now, in 1913, the Bishop wrote: 'You will see by the enclosed that I was quite correct that Seward himself had supplied the measurements of the site to Mr Haslewood, and the

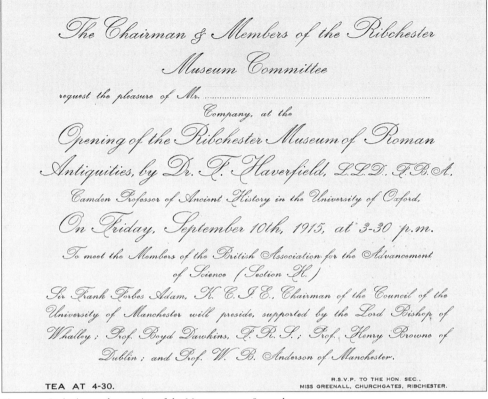

The Chairman & Members of the Ribchester Museum Committee

request the pleasure of Mr. ....

Company, at the

Opening of the Ribchester Museum of Roman Antiquities, by Dr. F. Haverfield, L.L.D., F.B.A.

Camden Professor of Ancient History in the University of Oxford,

On Friday, September 10th, 1915, at 3-30 p.m.

To meet the Members of the British Association for the Advancement of Science (Section H.)

Sir Frank Forbes Adam, K.C.I.E., Chairman of the Council of the University of Manchester will preside, supported by the Lord Bishop of Whalley; Prof. Boyd Dawkins, F.R.S.; Prof. Henry Browne of Dublin; and Prof. W. B. Anderson of Manchester.

TEA AT 4-30.   R.S.V.P. TO THE HON. SEC.,
MISS GREENALL, CHURCHGATES, RIBCHESTER.

Figure 27. Invitation to the opening of the Museum on 10 September, 1915.

conveyances had been drawn up on the basis of this survey'. Presumably Seward had used the incorrect measurements sent to him both for his own drawings and for submission to the solicitors for use in the conveyances.

1913 produced the usual problems with summer meetings, and an attempt made in June to arrange a meeting of the sub-Committee (as Col. Parker, the Bishop and Openshaw seem to have become) in July eventually resulted in a meeting in August. This considered Seward's Sketch Plan No. 3 of 1913 and resulted in a fourth plan by a day or two later. By the 22nd of August Plan No. 5 was being considered and the sixth and final plan of the year was submitted on 30th August.

This seems to have finally been acceptable, and in February of 1914 Miss Greenall sent three copies of the New Appeal to Col.

Parker. This apparently elicited a sharp reply from the colonel, for Miss Greenall wrote, on March 2nd, 1914, 'I have received your letter of the 27th and the corrected copy of the Appeal which I shall forward to Mr A. T. R. Houghton, Sec. of the Building Committee who got out the Appeal. I had nothing at all to do with any part of it and no proof was sent to me to see or correct. The Classical Association also sent out their appeal without consulting me. The Appeals were ordered to be sent to me to send out and I did not dare to question what the sub-Committee had done'. She went on to say 'We had a very successful meeting on Saturday ... The local tender was accepted and the School is to be demolished by the 25th of March'.

After all the delays, once work began it was

rapid. In early September, 1914, Miss Greenall was able to tell Col. Parker that 'the Parish Hall is quite ready for the Slates and the Museum will be ready for the roof timber early next week'. This was in the course of a letter in which she told him that the funds stood at £900, and the Bishop of Whalley wanted her to find six guarantors of £100 each to allow the work to be finished. His Lordship himself would be one, Miss Greenall's brother (by then in India) another; and, together with Col. Parker himself, Mr Openshaw and, possibly, Mr Simpson formed the six. A. T. R. Houghton, who had become treasurer of the Committee in April, had had to resign as he had rejoined the Loyal North Lancs. Regt. on the outbreak of war, and was at Swindon.

Photographs taken in 1914 show that archaeological work took place on the site of the old Sunday School. As usual, there are debit and credit sides to the way in which this happened. On the credit side is the fact that demolition seems to have been by hand. Where today mechanical equipment would be used, both the lack of suitable machinery and the proximity of the building to Churchgates (much nearer than the present Parish Hall) precluded that. Secondly, the photographs show that Roman walls survived four or more courses high (it is difficult to distinguish Roman floors and thus identify foundation courses) and the highest courses were little more than the depth of a spade blade below the old school floor. The excavations were carried out while much of the building was still standing. On the debit side there is first the state of archaeological technique at that date. The work was carried out by unskilled (in the archaeological sense) labour varying in age from a lad who cannot have been long out of school to a greybeard who was presumably 'the gaffer'. He, however, had been May's foreman in the Churchgates operation, John Hallows, and it is possible that some of the others had had similar experience.

It is also highly probable that the archaeological supervision was minimal, May's thoroughness being a rarity at that date. Finally, we must remember that no plan of the discoveries seems to have been made. At any rate, none has apparently survived, and certainly none has been published. What other deficiencies there may have been we do not know, but in her letter of September 8th, 1914, thanking Col. Parker for agreeing to be one of the guarantors for £100, Miss Greenall wrote: 'Yes, the excavations were not satisfactory and it was unfortunate that Mr May could not see his way to conduct them when the Sec. of the Classical Association asked him if he would kindly do so – later he changed his mind and rather regretted not having acceded to their request'. She went on to give several interesting pieces of information in a slightly enigmatic sentence. Having first agreed with Col. Parker, as we have seen, that the excavations were 'not satisfactory', she changed her tune slightly to say 'to me [they] were not so very disappointing, because I knew the old building was erected, possibly in 1500, as a malt kiln and that there was an underground furnace under the west end floor and that would necessitate the removal of any Roman remains, bases of columns, the foundations of which were found last Easter'. I presume this to mean that she thought the late medieval construction of the furnace *would already* have removed Roman remains *such as* those found at Easter.

She went on: 'The weather for the early part was exceedingly bad and the part which is to be excavated at Christmas will, I hope, be more fruitful, but was covered with tons of stone from the walls of the old building'. This rather suggests a three-part operation, which may have been devised to fit in with Donald Atkinson's vacations. Atkinson, who took over when May declined, was, as we have seen, Research Fellow at University College, Reading.

Whatever the shortcomings of the excavation, the Museum itself was duly opened on

September 15th, 1915. The opening ceremony was performed by Professor Francis Haverfield, and the function was combined with a visit of the Archaeological Section of the British Association for the Advancement of Science, then meeting in Manchester. Earlier, the Bishop of Whalley and Miss Greenall were signatories to a printed letter explaining that for the opening and for six montths afterwards the Museum's own collection was to be supplemented with 'a temporary Loan Exhibition of Roman objects found at Ribchester but now dispersed in other Museums or in private ownership'. The Committee hoped to hear of such objects. The writers hopefully added a sentence to the effect that the estimated cost of the Museum was £320, of which £150 had still to be raised.

To return to the opening ceremony, to which we have already referred: the chair was taken by Sir Frank Forbes Adam, Vice-Chancellor of Manchester University. Sir Frank is reported as having begun by refusing to apologise for holding such a gathering 'amidst the horrors and sorrows of war'. After a predictable sideswipe at Germany, he went on to give cogent reasons for the desirability of such a museum as that at Ribchester. Then, perhaps less predictably, he ascribed some of the success of the Roman Empire to the establishment in parts thereof of 'local self government'. Having made this point, he drew a a parallel with what he saw as similar activities within the British Empire, but noted that one colony without such institutions was India, 'peculiarly a country where we must go slowly and cautiously'. He went on, however, to say that 'the splendid exhibition of loyalty on the part of the princes and people of that dependency during the last twelve months would make it certain that, as soon as the war was over, a great effort would be made to advance one more important step towards the goal that everybody who loved India had in view'.

Coming back to more immediate matters, Sir Frank 'congratulated the Bishop of Whalley on the distinction recently conferred by the King on his son, and expressed the hope that his Lordship's other son, who had been

Figure 28. Seward's drawing of the then proposed Parish Hall and Museum, 1914.

taken prisoner at the Dardanelles, would soon return safe and well'. Haverfield then performed the opening ceremony and a general vote of thanks was proposed by the Bishop.

Printed copies of the Museum's first two sets of annual reports and accounts provide an interesting insight into the Museum's early days. In the first month of the Museum's opening, no fewer than 642 visitors were recorded, but, as the report suggests, the war probably contributed to the lower numbers in 1916, only 604 visitors being recorded in the whole of July, August and September of that year, although the highest number on a single day was the 59 of September 9th. The charge for visitors was 3d. per head, although soldiers in uniform were admitted free.

Admission fees, too, tell their tale. 1916 yielded nearly £14 10s., while 1917 did not quite manage £12. The last three and a half months of 1915 produced £8 1s. 5d., while the last three months of 1916 managed only 6s. 3d. The expenditure items for the two years are a little curious. The earlier breaks down into nearly £10 of non-recurring items together with £1 6s. 7d. for coal and oil for heating and lighting and £1 17s. 7d. for cleaning and weeding. £5 rent for the excavated area was paid to the Rector in each year, and 1916–17 yielded a credit balance of £4 7s. 9½d. In contrast, the only recorded expenditure for 1917 was 17s. 6d. for the printing of the last report and 11s. 4d. for two non-recurring items. The answer to the apparent puzzles in these accounts is, at least partially, to be found in the accompanying report: 'As labour was difficult to obtain, the task of cleaning the excavated area was carried out privately by the instructions of the Hon. Secretary, to whom the Committee is indebted for having most kindly borne the whole cost of the work'. This is a revealing sidelight on the effects of the First World War on village life, and presumably means that Miss Greenall persuaded her own domestic staff to come to the Museum's aid. The lack of lighting and heating costs remains unexplained.

The difficulty of obtaining labour presumably also accounts for the lack of trace in the 1917 accounts of an item twice referred to in 1916. 'The Committee arranged that the Museum should be open to the public on Thursdays and Saturdays and at such other times as the Hon. Secretary found convenient, the two days named being half-holidays in the neighbouring towns. Experience has shown that with such a rule those interested in Roman Antiquities visited Ribchester almost daily, the result being that the Hon. Secretary was called upon to permit access to the Museum daily save on Sundays. In future, during the brighter months of the year, a caretaker will be needed, as it is impossible for the Hon. Secretary to continue personally to admit all visitors to the Museum. As the public cannot be admitted without some responsible supervision, this duty has sometimes resulted in several hours per day being occupied'. This describes a situation familiar to all voluntary curators/caretakers, and one experienced again in recent years. 'The Honorary Secretary was however authorized to employ a caretaker subject to a maximum cost of 3s. per week'; this should have solved the problem.

These accounts were, of course, solely related to the costs of *running* the Museum. The reports which accompany them refer in both cases to the cost of *building* the Museum. The earlier one quotes the cost of erecting the Museum at £430 17s. 11d., of which £112 9s. 9d. was still outstanding. The bank interest was evidently calculated on the joint loan for building both parish Hall and Museum, and then apportioned by the Committee. Sums to reduce the Museum's part of the loan seem to have been sought only by donation – no part of the Museum's visitor income being dedicated to it. As a result, the interest had barely been covered and the principal had been reduced only by 3s. 6d.

The 1917 report and accounts had not appeared until March, 1918, a circumstance which Miss Greenall attributed to 'the press', presumably meaning a dilatory printer. Later in the same year a balance sheet for the entire project (Parish Hall and Museum) was produced. These accounts, covering the ten years from June, 1908 to June, 1918, reveal some interesting facts.

By the end of the period, £1715 had been spent, allocated as £1234 to the Parish Hall, £450 to the Museum and £31 to 'Excavations and Publication'. Of this sum, £1289 had been received in contributions, leaving a debt, at June 30th, 1918, of £426, allocated as £380 to the Parish Hall and £46 to the Museum. (All figures have been rounded). In her accompanying letter of 12th August, 1918, Miss Greenall said that the debts had been further reduced by £100 in the case of the Parish Hall and £3 in the case of the Museum.

The sources of the contributions are interesting. Only five individuals are recorded as contributing £10 or more to the Parish Hall as against ten to the Museum. One of the 'individuals' was in fact Miss Greenall and her brother, who gave £91 to the total sum, the allocation giving £22 to the Parish Hall and £69 to the Museum. Only three other people gave more than £20 to the total project, all of these sums being allotted to the Museum.

The big difference between the funding of the two parts of the project came with the holding of sales of work, socials and the like, which raised nearly half the total receipts -£614 – all allocated to the Parish Hall. Just what sad story may be concealed in the entry among these, 'Band; Social and Sale of Instruments', I do not know. The personal contributions to the Museum fund, by contrast, were augmented only by £51 in donations received by Miss Greenall 'when showing Roman antiquities', £9 in donations received by Mr Jas. Greenall and £11 for 'sale of pamphlets "Roman Ribchester"', presumably Hopkinson's reports.

The gallant ten who contributed £10 or more to the Museum were: Sir F. Forbes Adam (£10); J. R. Barlow (£27 10s.); Hy. Harrison (£29 10s.); Jesse Haworth (£25);

Sir Wm. Mather (£10); Col J. W. R. Parker (£10); Lord Shuttleworth (£10); W. W. Simpson (£10); H. Worrall (£10); Geo. Whittle (£10), together with the Roman Studies Society, which contributed £20.

It is no disrespect to the shade of Miss Greenall, but a corrective to the widely-held belief that she paid for the Museum, to point out that the entire sum, including donations, raised by the Greenalls covered less than one third of the cost of the Museum, the actual family contribution amounting to no more than 17% of it. These observations must by no means be taken to be derogatory. They present a financial state of of affairs which is incontrovertible. Besides, they in no way diminish the importance of another state of affairs: without Miss Greenall's idea of excavation concurrent with the creation of Churchgates and without her drive and vision, there would be no Museum at Ribchester, and little to put in one.

We have been able to follow the events leading up to, and immediately following, the establishment of the Museum in some detail thanks to the fortuitous survival of documentary evidence. After the First World War, this type of evidence has not been preserved, and indeed, such a detailed consideration of the Museum's history throughout the succeeding eighty years would not be justified, even if the evidence were available. Nevertheless, it is desirable to give a short summary of events.

We have seen that the foundation of the Museum included the conveying of the land to the National Trust, which had been in existence only since 1895. The arrangement whereby the National Trust were the owners, and the management of the Museum was in the hands of a Local Committee, continued until 1989, when a local Trust took over the running of the Museum. The problem from the point of view of the National Trust was the two-fold one of scale (Ribchester Museum is a very small operation in terms of finance and visitor numbers, and correspondingly expensive to run) and of the

Figure 29. Photograph of the newly-opened Museum with its first custodian, Richard Barton, outside. (Photograph by Buck of Clitheroe, courtesy of Mrs Ena Jones. Buck also produced a version of this photograph with the figure scratched off the negative.).

financial reality that Ribchester was a net loss-maker to the National Trust.

The displays in the Museum's early days were, by modern standards, obviously crude, but many of the exhibits can be recognised in early photographs. The first Curator of the Museum (presumably the 'caretaker' of the 1917 annual report) was Richard Barton, who had taken part in the excavation of the schoolroom area. His niece, Mrs Ena Jones, who is still living in Ribchester, has recalled that on the opening day of the Museum, described above, there was a marquee on the Rectory lawn.

Of the remainder of the period between the wars little is now recorded. At one stage the Museum was looked after by Miss Phyllis Sidebotham, daughter of the Rector (1924–1943). She was succeeded by Miss Hindshaw, who had been Curator of the now-defunct Horsfall Museum in Manchester. While there is no doubt that some of her ideas were

unusual, she was in advance of her time in that she made considerable attempts to cater for children, providing small peep-show dioramas and a model of the Roman Wall (whether Hadrian's or that at Ribchester does not seem to be clear) in the garden. Attempts were made to assist her by asking the Assistant Curator of the Harris Museum and Art Gallery in Preston, Mrs Tyson, to visit. She has recorded that these visits resulted in little in the way of assistance as Miss Hindshaw regarded them as purely social.

They did have one important result, however, for when Miss Hindshaw left, after the death of a sister, in 1954, the post was offered to Mrs Tyson herself. She was a Museums Association Diploma holder, but by then had a small child, and the offer of the Museum Cottage and £52 *per annum* was sufficient to tempt her, opportunities for work for mothers with small children being then much more limited than they are today.

Figure 30. Early photographs of the interior of the Museum.

Mrs Tyson carried out a number of schemes of improvement, removing much material of inferior standard (the dioramas, for example, and the Roman Wall model) and much non-local material. Under her Curatorship the granaries, much neglected and overgrown, were re-excavated and consolidated and a complete refitting of the Museum to the design of Mr Frank Lord was carried out with the aid of a Carnegie Trust grant. Well-known figures were involved with these proceedings, the re-excavation of the granaries being supervised by Mr Brian Hartley of Leeds, the subsequent re-instatement of the site by Sir Ian Richmond, and the report which led to the obtaining of the Carnegie grant being written by Dr Donald Harden.

On Mrs Tyson's move from Ribchester to Lancaster Museum in 1965, the next Curator was Mrs N. Dixon, who remained until 1982. Much was done in and around the Museum during her tenure, with a flourishing local archaeological society as one of its chief arms. Although the Museum was relatively newly refurbished when Mrs Dixon took over, it soon became apparent that lack of space was a considerable hindrance to development.

The answer to this problem was the provision, behind the 1914 building, of a prefabricated extension. Not long after this, a similar extension was added to the kitchen of the cottage, behind the Museum. This gave both the Museum and its Curator reasonable space.

Buildings of this type, however, have a limited life, and it became apparent by 1989 that both were in need of replacement. In the scheme ultimately adopted, the Museum cottage became part of the Museum and a two-storey extension was built in place of the temporary structure behind the Museum, Mrs Dixon having moved out of the cottage into a bungalow in the village some time before, and having resigned as Curator in 1982. The Museum which resulted from the addition of the new building is L-shaped, and its initial display scheme was a completely new concept. The Museum was, however, without a Curator, and the expenditure of funds necessitated by the new building and the new displays meant that the money to employ one was not available. We saw how, in its earliest days, the Museum placed great demands on its amateur custodian, and the Committee were now aware that to expect such unrewarded service was both

unreasonable and unlikely to be possible. However, as so often in the history of the Museum, the situation was saved by the appearance of the right person at the right time. Mr J. F. Ridge, a Preston history teacher with a long involvement with Ribchester, had moved into the village on taking early retirement, and for several years he acted as Honorary Curator.

Although the new plans provided a storeroom to allow a growing collection of non-display finds to be housed, this aspect of the Museum's activity was insufficiently catered for, and it is being addressed at the time of writing, under the direction of another professional Curator. Mr P. Tostevin came to the Museum in 1993, and, in addition to overseeing the achievement of the Museum's registration by the Museums and Galleries Commission, has vastly increased the educational dimension of its work. This being a work of record rather than a promotional report, it is not the place to describe the Museum's future plans; but it will suffice to say that it is hoped that it will continue to be both a specialist institution for those interested in Roman Britain and, increasingly, an important element in the tourism element of the village's life.

CHAPTER EIGHT

The helmet and its associated finds

In 1796 Thomas Dunham Whitaker, who lived at a house called The Holme in Cliviger, heard of a discovery which had been made in the village of Ribchester. One of the village's tradesmen was its clogger and shoemaker, a man called Joseph Walton, and he lived in the last house on the western side of the main street leading down to the river. For reasons which we are not told, his son John, who was thirteen at the time, was digging in a hollow in a piece of waste ground behind his house, and made a discovery. Again, we do not know exactly what the young John found, for his father took over, and it was he who gradually amassed a group of Roman objects.

When Whitaker told his friend Charles Townley of Towneley Hall about the discovery, Townley decided to buy the objects from Joseph Walton. This was over a year after the actual discovery, and there had been time for at least one of the objects, said to have been a sphinx, to have been passed to Joseph Walton's brother, Lawrence, and for it to have been lost by his children.

Townley, however, bought 32 items , and it is sad that we have no record of what he paid for them. He was familiar with the process of purchasing antiquities, for he had a large collection mainly acquired in Italy, though many of these had been bought for him by agents. This collection was housed in his London house at Park Street (now Queen Anne's Gate), Westminster, and was available to be viewed by the public. A catalogue existed, though only in manuscript, and the collection was also the subject of a well-known picture, 'Charles Townley among his Marbles', by the best-known society painter of the day, Johann Zoffany. The painting is now in Towneley Hall Art Gallery, Burnley, and is idealised in the sense that not all the objects shown in it were ever in the same room together. Indeed, for artistic purposes Zoffany took such liberties as placing sculptures on bookcases which could not have supported them, or reducing the size of a statue in order to include it without allowing it to dominate the scene.

We do not know that the Ribchester objects, of which by far the most important is a Roman cavalry parade helmet, were ever displayed in London. They did, however, inspire Charles Townley to do something he did not do for the rest of his collection – that is to publish an account of them. The idea of doing that sort of thing was relatively new. True, the Royal Society had been publishing its *Philosophical Transactions* for scientific papers since 1665, but it had had few imitators. The Society of Antiquaries of London, founded in 1718, had begun a journal called *Archaeologia, or Miscellaneous Tracts relating to Antiquity* in 1770. Townley, or someone at the Society, however, felt that a better means of publishing the Ribchester objects existed, this being an irregularly issued serial known as *Vetusta Monumenta*. The advantage of this over *Archaeologia* was its very large page size (17½ in. × 22 in.), which meant that illustrations could often be at or near life size.

The obtaining of illustrations of the Ribchester objects presented no great difficulty. The Society of Antiquaries had its own artist, the senior member of a dynasty of three all called James Basire. The four plates of the Ribchester finds were drawn by several artists, but all engraved by Basire.

Figure 31. The Ribchester parade helmet. (Photograph courtesy of the British Museum).

Townley, however, had no experience of writing an account of a discovery such as that at Ribchester. The idea of the scientific paper as we now know it had not yet been born, and accounts such as Townley was to write were couched in the form of a letter to the President or Secretary of the society which was to publish it. In the case we are considering, Townley's letter was ostensibly addressed to the Secretary of the Society of Antiquaries, John Brand. This is of interest because, by a remarkable chance, the manuscript of Townley's paper has survived, and it is possible to discern Brand's hand (or at least that of someone of experience) in the numerous re-writings and alterations in it.

That it was the experienced author Brand who helped Townley is to be deduced from the increasingly complimentary references to Brand's own *History of Newcastle*, then recently published. Much as one would like to think that Whitaker had a hand in matters, it must be remembered that he had not yet published his first book.

We have considered some of the subsidiary aspects of what I have called the Ribchester Hoard, but we ought now to return to the beginning and describe what was found. The first notice of it to reach the general public was in the *Blackburn Mail* of 3 August, 1796. This reads as follows:- 'A few days ago some ancient figures etc. were discovered in a scar on the Ribble side near Ribchester, a few miles from this place, about 9 feet below the surface of the earth. The river had washed part of them there, which induced the persons who discovered them to dig up the earth, where they found a metal helmet or cap-a-pie, embellished with a number of small figures of men on horseback, with swords in their hands; also some small figures or busts in relievo; and a red earthen dish, which holds about three quarts, having a pouring spout, and a rim round it, on which are the initials B. O. R. J. E. D. F. with a number of small metal dishes; an oak chair having the remains of a leather bottom, and a quantity of old leather lying near it; and different other matters – the whole of which are now in the possession of a person at Ribchester. The kind of metal of which the figures are composed being of so high a colour is not yet perfectly known to the people there; and the person who sent this account is in doubt whether it may be gold. It is supposed by some discerning persons that they must have lain there some hundred years'.

This is a very interesting account because, although brief and incomplete, it is immediate, and not subject to the revisions which Townley chose to make later. Several facts which are mentioned in the full account are already stated in the newspaper account. For

example, the depth is given correctly, and the figures on the helmet are mentioned, while the stamp on the mortarium is almost exactly correct, if we ignore the full stops. Bearing this in mind, the description of the wood and leather as being like a chair with a leather bottom and with old leather nearby may suggest some form of container and/or harness. The fact that the full account describes the find as having been made in a cube of sand suggests the shape for a box or chest. The newspaper account also speaks of the paper's correspondent wondering if the objects which we know to have been of bronze were in fact of gold, which makes us think that the soil conditions were, as so often in Ribchester, conducive to the good preservation of metals.

What in fact had Joseph Walton discovered and Townley bought? First, and most important, the cavalry parade helmet. This is one of about sixty similar objects known from the Roman Empire, of which four or five come from Britain. It is, however, the one which has caught the imagination of writers and particularly of artists. Almost any general account of Roman Britain is likely to have an illustration of it, and general descriptions of Roman cavalry frequently use it also. We will defer a slightly more detailed consideration of its characteristics in order to describe briefly the objects which accompanied it. There were, first, several of the metal discs with loops on the reverse which made up the harness of a Roman cavalryman's horse. They were functional in that they enabled two or more straps to join, and they were also treated decoratively. There were also two pierced hemispherical objects which were the eye-guards originally attached to the leather head-piece of a cavalry horse.

It is extremely tantalising to realise that had the find been made in recent years, we might well have the entire harness of a cavalryman's horse. As it is, there are one or two peculiarities about what we do and do not have. For example, the strap junction plates to which reference has already been made

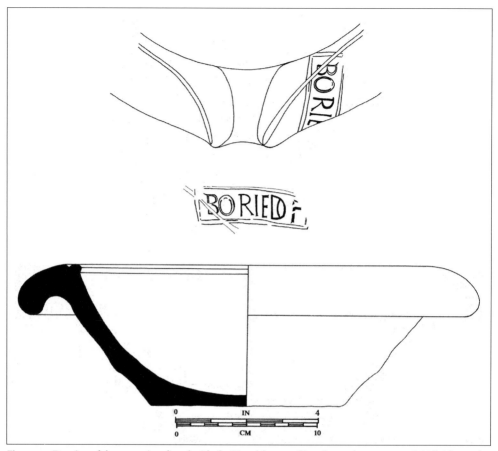

Figure 32. Drawing of the *mortarium* found with the Hoard in 1796. (Drawing author, courtesy British Museum).

usually had decorative pendants hanging from them. There are undoubtedly fewer than a full set of these plates, but even so, one might have expected a pendant or two to have survived, but there is no such object present. It might be as well here to draw attention to the difference between the making of a find such as that we are discussing in the course of a modern archaeological excavation and what would have occurred at the end of the eighteenth century. It is highly unlikely that any great care was taken to be sure that every piece of material was recovered. Certainly such things as the wood of the 'chair' and the leather would have been almost completely disregarded, and no

attempt would have been made to observe details accurately. So the presence or absence of expected items means little. The 'sphinx' was lost by Joseph Walton's nephew and niece; it is not improbable that, in the year between the finding of the hoard and Townley's buying it, other items were not kept too carefully. And the fact that Townley makes no mention of the 'chair' and its associated leather probably means that no-one remembered to tell him about them.

Again, although the helmet is present, no other part of the horseman's own accoutrements is present. The eye-guards have been explained, not least by the present writer, as having fitted into a leather *chamfrein* or *chamfron* of the type found at Newstead in Scotland at the beginning of the century and, in part, at Ribchester itself in recent years, as well as at *Vindolanda*. Nevertheless, it must be admitted that the sizes of the eye-guards and holes in the leather chamfrons do not exactly match.

There were other objects – three of the bronze camp kettles or skillets used by Roman soldiers, one of them a very shallow example, another fragmentary, but all with the complex ringed bases which look as though they were designed for heat efficiency. One or two of the objects may not have been truly associated with the main find, which surely must have been buried as a means of safeguarding the objects. The *mortarium* (mixing bowl), for example, may simply have been lost in the area in which the deposit was made – though its being complete suggests that it may indeed belong with the deposit. There seems also to have been a dish-like object allegedly made of wood, which the writer has suggested may actually have been of shale, a soft rock freely used for ornaments by the Romans. Most shale objects were lathe-turned, but free-carved objects are known.

Townley wrote up his purchase, and his account is illustrated with two plates of the helmet and two of other objects. It is in the preparation of these illustrations that we can observe several interesting facets of Townley at work. In the first place, he insisted that the engraver should indicate where parts of the objects were restored. He was not entirely successful in this. For example, the harness plates were shown as complete and undamaged, which was almost certainly not the case. They must, in any case, have been somewhat corroded, for their quite delicate incised decoration is not shown.

Townley's attitude to the matter of restoration was unusual at the time. Artists restored ancient objects in their illustrations without comment, but the treatment of the helmet in particular shows that Townley would not countenance such deception.

Among the main illustrations there is a full-face view of the helmet. It should be explained that the helmet itself was in two separate pieces – the cap and the face-mask. The upper part of the latter, between the eyebrows and the hair line, carries decoration which consists of a turretted wall with panelled decoration, with the decoration of the panels roughly matching to left and right of the centre. In the centre was a panel which had been completely broken away before the helmet was found. In the engraving this central panel was left undecorated, being merely shaded.

We do know, however, that Townley was tempted to add decoration, for there survives in the British Museum a sheaf of small pieces of paper, pinned together, on which he has drawn possible decorations for this central panel. In fact this little piece of evidence of Townley's methods is only part of a surprising amount of documentation relating to the publication of the Ribchester Hoard. The British Museum also has an invaluable little plan, in Townley's own hand, which disposes once and for all of any doubt as to the whereabouts of the findspot. Townley himself drew and had engraved a view of the 'diadem' of the helmet, as the brow portion became known. This was labelled 'The Diadem expanded, and shown in its mutilated State, to authorize the Reparations given in the preceding Plates'. Finally, the manuscript of the text, already mentioned, is in the Harris Library in Preston, while the British Museum has a fair copy of this, which was almost certainly the text used by the printer.

It is worth adding a few words about the decoration of the helmet. In the classification of helmets of this type published by a competent writer (Robinson 1975), there are only three of the particular group represented by the Ribchester helmet. The characteristic which they share is the possession of an up-turned peak looking rather like that of a jockey's cap. The other two helmets come, one from Newstead, Scotland, and the other

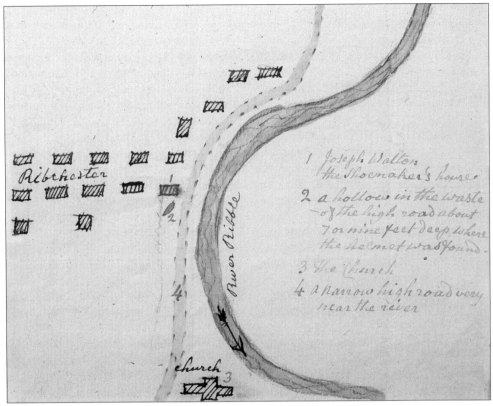

Figure 33. Charles Townley's plan to show the find-spot of the Hoard. (Courtesy British Museum).

from Nikopolis, on the River Jantra in Bulgaria. The peaks of these helmets have protrusions on their edge, and the Ribchester one is unique in that the two protrusions nearest to the wearer's ears are cut in the outline shape of dolphins. There is no other aquatic element in the decoration of the cap of the helmet, as opposed to the face-mask. The remainder of the decoration of the cap consists of sixteen figures of armed men. Some are depicted in armour, some naked; some carry spears, some swords; some are on foot, some ride. They are often described as a battle scene, and indeed such they may be intended to recall. But in fact, though all are fighting, they are not fighting each other. There seems to be a strong probability that the dies with which they were raised were designed to form a battle scene, but on the

helmet they are randomly disposed – so randomly that at least one soldier is seated, but has nothing on which to sit !

The obvious question raised by this discovery is that of the reason for the presence in the ground of this collection of objects. We cannot, obviously, know the answer to that with certainty. When it comes to speculation, there are facts which we can take into consideration. Firstly, the find is not unique. There are quite a number of similar finds of Roman armour, associated with other things, from widely-spread parts of the Empire. This does not, of course, mean that the reason for their deposition is necessarily the same in all cases. However, we might reasonably guess that the motives for most of such deposits are similar. Usually, it is accepted that depositing in the ground in the

Figure 34. *Carte de visite* (?) of Charles Townley, drawn and engraved by W. Skelton. (Courtesy Towneley Hall Museum, Burnley).

past of items of value was due to the existence of some threat which the owner of the objects wished to avoid – and this is usually interpreted as something like enemy action. But the idea that someone might wish to deprive an owner of what was rightfully his is not the only possibility. It is quite possible, for example, that the objects were buried by someone who had no right to them – a thief, in fact. Presumably the fact that they were still there to be found nearly two millennia later implies that the last possessor of them, rightful or otherwise, was not in a position finally to recover them.

The possibility of accidental loss is much more difficult to support. That individual items were often lost is clear. Apart from finds of such objects as coins, brooches, tools – in fact the contents of an archaeological Small Finds report – there are examples where the reason for the loss can actually be demonstrated. Two at least of the bronze arm-purses from sites on Hadrian's Wall, for instance, were found where the circumstances made it clear that they had been put down by soldiers working on rampart-building, and then covered in the building process. Entirely explicable and understandable, one might say. However, the Ribchester hoard was in a cube of sand, possibly representing a container, measuring a yard in each dimension. This, unlike the purses, was not something which could have been easily forgotten or accidentally covered. Furthermore, the find-spot was clearly near the fort rampart, which would provide an excellent hiding-place for something so bulky. It seems, then, that of our two options, we must envisage deliberate burial; but there is no means of discriminating between burial by a lawful owner in circumstances of fear, and burial by a thief. Perhaps one might add that the latter is more likely, in that a soldier might hide his pay or other valuables in an emergency, but surely not his equipment.

One final point is worth mentioning. The helmet bears *graffiti* – that is unofficial inscriptions – on both the cap and the face mask. They were inscibed by the use of a punch, and are presumably ownership marks. They were not noticed until 1960, but the name they record, CARAVI, is known within the Roman Empire only from Spain. Is there a hint here of a connection between the hoard and the Asturian garrison ? (See also Edwards 1992, Edwards in Edwards and Webster (eds) forthcoming, and Jackson and Craddock 1995).

CHAPTER NINE

Sculptured stones and other finds

It is one of the tenets of the archaeologist that 'finds' are only a part of the evidence which he gathers in order to illuminate the particular period of the past with which he is concerned; and, in particular, that finds need to be considered *in their context* in order to yield the maximum amount of evidence. There is, therefore, a tendency to be a little shamefaced about interest in finds for their own sake, despite the fact that many archaeologists were attracted to the subject in the first place by finding a fascination in one or more class of finds. The following descriptions of some of the more interesting of the finds from the Roman period is offered without apology, because the subject matter is intrinsically interesting.

Stone

The cavalry tombstone

This, one of the most prominent objects in the museum, is at the same time one of the more enigmatic. It was found on the left bank of the river to the east of the fort in 1876, and is one of a well-known class of tombstone known as the 'rider and barbarian' type. A study of 134 Roman tombstones showing cavalrymen on horeseback, from all over the Empire (Schleiermacher 1984), divided them into four classes according to whether the soldier was galloping or stationary and whether or not a barbarian (*gegner* – enemy) was present on the stone. This study showed very clearly that the 'rider and barbarian' type is commonest in Britain, with a few examples from the Rhineland and Gaul, in the first century, and, assuming that the

dating is accurate, that the type spreads as far east as Thrace and Macedonia and also into North Africa in the second, third and fourth centuries. The Ribchester stone differs from most in that it lacks the usual funerary inscription, and on that account doubt has even been thrown on its status as a tombstone. It is well known that Roman sculptures and inscriptions were painted, and that errors in carved inscriptions were probably corrected in paint. To suggest, as has been done, that the Ribchester stone either had a painted inscription alone, or that the inscription relating to it was on another stone, takes one into areas where it is very difficult to cite other examples. Equally uncertain and productive of controversy is the suggestion that the rider shown was one of the Asturian garrison of the fort, and the speculation, if so, as to whether or not the appearance of the rider provides any real evidence of the appearance of such soldiers. As in all such cases, there cannot have been any glaring error which would have led a contemporary viewer to ridicule the carving; similarly, the appearance of the soldier may have been no more than that of a generalised cavalryman.

The Apollo Maponus stone

The stone carrying the inscription to Apollo Maponus (that is the Apollo of Classical legend assimilated to the Celtic god Mabon) has been recorded for three hundred years longer than the cavalry tombstone. It was first noted at Salesbury Old Hall by William Camden. His description sounds as though he saw only the side with the inscription (which he called the 'backe side or reverse') and the 'front', which, he said, had '*Cupide*

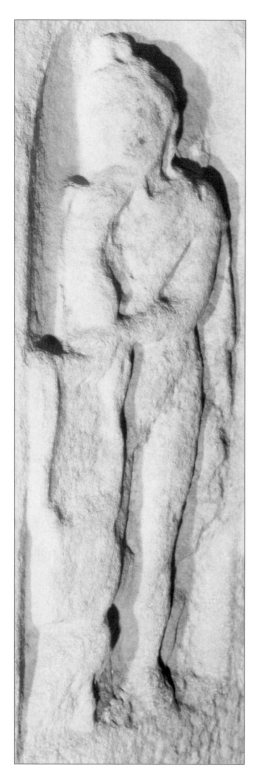

Figure 35. The figures of Apollo/Maponus and two
female personifications from the Apollo/Maponus
base.

and another little image'. He made no mention of the other obvious sculpture, of Apollo, and it raises the possibility that at that time the stone was built into a wall with two sides visible and the other two hidden. By the late eighteenth century it was incorporated in a corner of the Hall and thence it was removed in 1814 at the request of Thomas Dunham Whitaker, who obtained the stone and bequeathed it with others to his college, St John's at Cambridge, by the permission of whose governing body it (and they) are on display at the Museum. The carving on two of the surviving sides and the inscription on the other make it a very interesting stone indeed. Apollo with his lute and quiver is reasonably obvious; but the two draped figures are less easily explained. Richmond thought that they represented two female figures of which one wore a mural crown, thereby identifying herself as symbolic of a place. The other represented the region in which that place lay, and the object between the figures an item representing a privilege being granted by the latter to the former. Richmond even considered that he could detect the symbolic or mock rejection of the privilege by the recipient. True or not, this view does not explain the function of the stone itself. There is a fairly large socket on its upper surface, and it has been called a statue base. Dedicated as it is to Apollo, whose representation is on one side, it can hardly have been the base for a statue of that god. Its general appearance, with reliefs under arches, recalls the bases of Jupiter giant columns in the Rhineland, and the suggestion is here offered that it may have carried some form of column rather than a statue. Other instances are known from Britain of the assimilation of the gods Apollo and Mabon/Maponus, for example, from Corbridge and from an uncertain site further west, on Hadrian's Wall.

[For the inscription on this stone see p. 87]

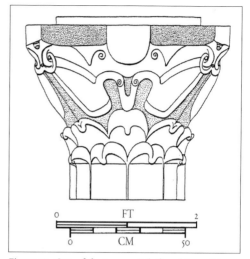

Figure 36. One of the two capitals found in 1908 in the filling of a well. They represent a 'military simplification' of the Corinthian order.

The column capitals

When Thomas May was excavating the headquarters building of the fort in 1906–8, he found three wells, and in the third of these there were a number of stones from columns. These included two large Corinthian capitals which are now in the Museum. They are simpler in design than most Corinthian capitals, and it has been suggested that they represent a specifically military type of design, though it has also been said that this is more likely to be due to the desire for cheapness than any artistic considerations. They have been compared to capitals from the legionary fortress at Chester, and assigned to a 'Wroxeter-Chester-Ribchester' school of sculpture, which is presumably to be connected with the Twentieth Legion, which we know to have worked at Ribchester. Perhaps the most remarkable thing about these capitals is the sophistication which they imply in a remote auxiliary fort towards the extreme border of the Empire.

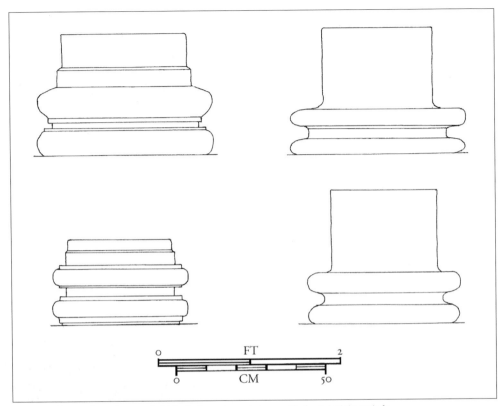

Figure 37. Four column bases, of which the largest may belong with the *principia* capitals.

Column bases

May also found a number of column bases, at least one of which may be from the same columns as the capitals. The others imply, of course, other colonnaded buildings at Ribchester apart from the headquarters building.

Other carved stones

These include part of a frieze with volutes; a pine-cone finial; stones which may have been statue bases; the possible base of a water-tank; a cylindrical stone with an end of smaller diameter, which bears comparison with a stone resting on the east abutment of the bridge over the North Tyne near Chesters on Hadrian's Wall. This, which also has a square base, is considered to have been part of the decoration on the bridge itself; was there a Roman bridge at Ribchester? In addition there are two small uninscribed altars (did they have painted inscriptions?); and, interestingly, a stone prepared for the reception of an inscription which was never added, unless it, too, was merely painted. This stone, which was found in the area of the Commander's house (*praetorium*) in 1970, retained parts of its moulded borders which showed that the maximum width of the lines of the inscription for which it was prepared was two feet (700 mm). Incised guide-lines for at least seven lines of text, each initally of just over 3¼ inches (84 mm) in height, were being cut, but the mason forgot to leave a space between the second and third lines of text.

He corrected this by inserting a space in such a way that these lines of text would have been only about 2¾ inches (70 mm) in height. We have no way of knowing, of course, whether or not this was the cause of the abandonment of the stone, and its use as a paving stone, as it was found. At any rate, the sharpness of the chisel marks strongly suggests that the stone had never been exposed to the weather.

Mention should be made here of the Roman altar which is preserved at the west end of the north aisle of Whalley church, some six miles from Ribchester and in the valley of the Ribble's tributary, the Calder. This stone is often described as having been brought from Ribchester, though there is no direct evidence of this. (There are two other stones at Whalley, one of which is certainly Roman (the inscription built in above the arch of the north doorway of the church – RIB 599) and another probably so (the large stone with a lewis-hole outside the south side of the tower). All may have come from Ribchester, though neither the altar nor the stone with the lewis-hole shows any sign of having been used as a building stone. Imprecise records of Roman coins from the churchyard may be thought to suggest, when taken with these three stones, the presence of a Roman site at or near Whalley.) To return to the altar: it shows a Roman soldier with sword, spear and round shield, and presumably implies a dedication to Mars. The unsophisticated nature of the carving perhaps suggests that this, too, was a case of Mars having been assimilated to a Celtic god, as he is known to have been, for example, to Thincsus at Housesteads or Coccidius at Bewcastle. Interestingly, although the head of the figure is damaged, it seems to have worn the type of tripartite 'jester's cap' seen on reliefs of Mars from Custom Scrubs, near Bisley, Gloucestershire (Toynbee 1963, No. 63, p. 152, pl. 65).

Another carved stone which we know to have come from Ribchester, although it is preserved even further from the site than Whalley , is the relief of a standard-bearer built in to a light-well at Standen Hall, near Clitheroe. This is recorded by Thomas Pennant as having been brought there by John Aspinall. There is a cast in the Museum.

Under this heading, too, must be included a number of artifacts of shale. This substance is known to have been worked by the Romans around Kimmeridge, in Dorset, and possibly elsewhere. Ribchester has yielded pieces of bracelets and the larger part of a carved dish remarkably similar to one found in the Isle of Wight.

Several intaglios, or ring settings, are among the finds from the site. One, inscribed AVE MEA VITA, has already been mentioned. This was recorded by Thomas Pennant 'in the possession of a poor man' and is said to have been of gold, the stone a cornelian cut into a hexagonal form with

Figure 38. Figure of a standard-bearer from Ribchester, built into Standen Hall, near Clitheroe.

Figure 39. Examples of engraved *intaglios*.

four of the sides longer than the other two. On the upper surface was engraved a bird. This ring was owned at one time by Thomas Dunham Whitaker and descended to his great grand-daughter, a Mrs Gillespie, who lived near Abergavenny and who supplied Watkin with the drawings on which his engraving was based. It would be fascinating if it were still somewhere in south Wales. Three other intaglios are illustrated here.

Domestic items

Like every other Roman site, Ribchester has produced many thousands of sherds of pottery and many hundreds of pieces of other materials, such as glass, bronze, iron, lead, wood, bone and even the occasional semi-precious stone in the form of a ring-setting. Most of these are run-of-the-mill, and require no comment here; frequently, their usefulness lies in the realm of dating, and here their numerousness and normality are important features. We shall have to wait for the appearance of the full report on the excavations in the churchyard extension to learn more of such objects as wooden combs and pieces of horse-harness (including parts of a *chamfron* like that from Newstead in southern Scotland). Nevertheless, there are in these categories one or two pieces which are worthy of comment, and they will be presented under the heading of the material, in the order given at the beginning of this paragraph.

Glass

No highly significant pieces. Part of one small cut beaker closely recalls one from Hardknott (Cumbria). Other pieces include counters or 'men' from board games, made

Figure 41. Spiral bronze wire brooch from the playing field excavations of 1969. A similar brooch came from the churchyard extension excavations.

by allowing a single large drop of molten glass to cool on a cold surface, producing a small plano-convex disc.

Bronze

Again nothing of outstanding interest. A spiral brooch found in 1969 is something of a rarity. Among other brooches from the site, one, a trumpet brooch, was said to have been of gold, but a case has been made out by the writer for this identification having been the result of a misinterpretation of a bronze brooch found in almost unweathered condition as a result of burial in anaerobic

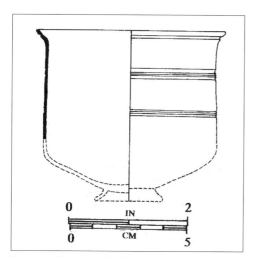

Figure 40. Drawing of a glass beaker from Ribchester, 1968.

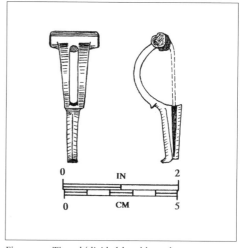

Figure 42. Tinned 'divided-bow' brooch.

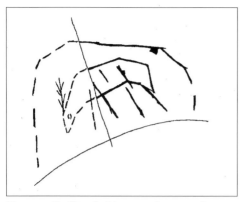

Figure 43. Graffito of a ?deer on a fragment of samian ware.

Figure 44. Part of a barrel found in a well in the course of the Sewerage works, 1974.

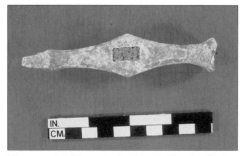

Figure 45. Small hammer-head, probably a jeweller's tool, from the churchyard extension excavations.

(oxygen-free) conditions (Edwards 1997). Among nineteenth century records of bronze objects is a steelyard (with lead weights) and there is a watercolour of another in the Binns Collection at Liverpool Library. A lead weight with double iron hook from yet another was found in the 1970s.

Lead

Apart from the steelyard weights just mentioned, and a number of pieces which must have been smaller balance weights, a curious object in this material was found when an archaeological assessment was carried out to the south of the bath-house. This object, better visualised from the illustration than from a description, bore a remarkable resemblance to the 'tamga' signs known to have been used by Sarmatians, and may well be connected with their time in garrison at Ribchester.

Iron

Ribchester is not particularly kind to buried iron. A piece found some years ago may be a window divider.

Wood

The lower levels at Ribchester are frequently waterlogged, and so quite good for the preservation of organic materials. The wattle wall found in the civilian settlement in 1969 has already been alluded to, and timber mortice-and-tenon joints were also found at the same time. The churchyard extension excavations produced large quantities of wood, and an appraisal of this will appear in the report of that excavation. One extremely interesting object of wood, found in the area of the school, was a spindle. Spindle-whorls of many materials, particularly stone, pottery and bone, are frequently found on Roman sites. The spindle on which they were mounted, and to which they gave the necessary weight to produce the rotary motion which imparted twist to the thread, is rarely preserved.

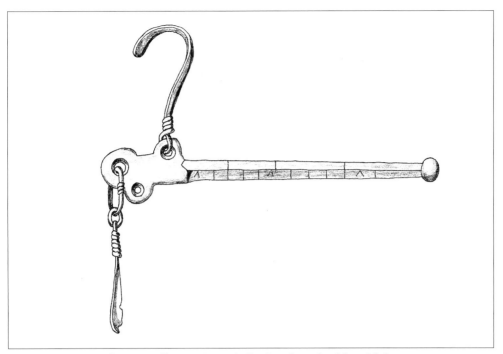

Figure 46. Drawing in the Binns Collection, Liverpool Libraries, of a steelyard from Ribchester.

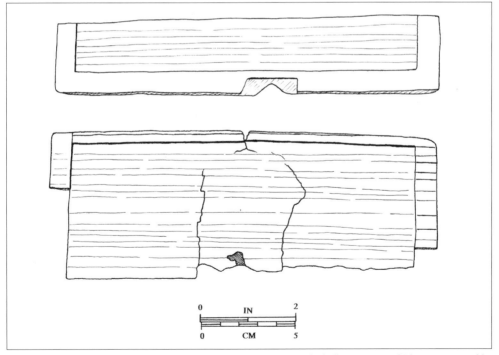

Figure 47. Two wooden writing tablets. These would have had wax in the hollow part, on which messages would be written with a *stylus*.

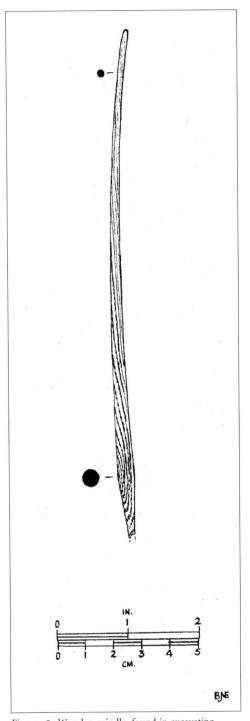

One of the sensations of Romano-British archaeology in recent decades has been the discovery of ink-inscribed birch writing tablets at *Vindolanda*, near Hadrian's Wall. No such tablet has been recovered at Ribchester, though the conditions in lower levels would favour their preservation. Writing tablets of the other common Roman type, however, in which the surface of a small flat piece of wood with a raised rim was covered with wax and the message inscribed thereon with a stylus, have been found, though none has had its message sufficiently firmly incised to leave a legible impression on the wood, as has happened elsewhere.

Bone

Counters for games closely resembling modern draughts, though much smaller, have been found. In addition, a casual find in the nineteenth century of a small carving, in bone, of two seated lions separated by a ?tree looks as though it came from the handle of a knife or some similar object.

Figure 48. Wooden spindle, found in excavating foundations for an extension to the school.

CHAPTER TEN

General Historical Summary

The village of Ribchester, we know, has attracted visitors for many years, and it is, of course, the presence there at one time of the Romans which largely accounts for this. Nevertheless, it is fair to say that it would be an attractive place for the visitor even without that special lure. We have seen(p. 9) that the name of the village indicates that there was a settlement there prior to the Norman Conquest, and there are a few tangible hints about this. Within the church there are two fragments of stone crosses which predate the Normans, though probably not by a great deal. The British Museum has a silver bracelet which is of the Saxon period and certainly came from the village. Ribchester Museum itself has a shield boss, a brooch and a couple of fragments of pottery which, if truly local finds, would indicate a much earlier Saxon presence. Unfortunately, there is no certainty that they were not gifts to the Museum, which had originated in, for example, East Anglia. It seems probable that, given the amount of excavation which has taken place at Ribchester, more pre-Conquest material would have been found if there had been extensive settlement at the time. One must not also overlook one or two coin finds, but these need mean no more than casual loss by visitors.

Just a hint of life at Ribchester between the Anglo-Saxons and the Normans is to be found in the illustration with which Watkin closed his Ribchester chapter. This was of a small bronze boss of probable Irish origin and ninth century date. Watkin knew it was not Roman, saying, 'though not belonging to the [Roman] period … it can scarcely be considered out of place … to introduce here an engraving of a very beautiful bronze boss, which was found at this station'. Sadly, it perished in the bombing of Liverpool Museum in 1941, but it is at least possible that it came from the grave of a Norseman in the churchyard.

Passing mention has also been made of the fact that there was some kind of occupation in the vicinity of Ribchester much earlier than the suggested Saxon village, which we presume is the direct ancestor of the present village. The Bronze Age burial urns discovered by accident in the course of the excavations on the site of the sheltered housing in Parsonage Avenue must indicate that people lived not very far away in the second millennium B.C.; however, we know comparatively little of the relationship between living sites and burial sites at the time.

Both the prehistoric occupation and the pre-Conquest occupation have left very little in the way of visible evidence, nor, indeed, as in most villages, has the earlier post-Conquest settlement. The chief evidence for this, of course, is the church, again in keeping with the majority of English villages. There was a Norman church, evidenced now only by a few sculptured stones within the present church. Most of that church, however, dates from the thirteenth century and later, and forms a body of implied evidence for the existence of the medieval village, evidence which does not exist elsewhere except in documents, and which is also largely lacking from excavations, though many of the latter have produced a certain amount of medieval pottery. The period of the village's history which is most vividly evoked by the village itself is the eighteenth century, from which time many of the houses must date, a fact often confirmed by the presence of datestones on the houses. At this time textiles were a source of prosperity to the village, and it is interesting to recall that Lawrence Walton, the uncle of the small boy who discovered the Ribchester helmet, was a calico weaver.

As in all villages, the nineteenth century wrought great changes, of which the most considerable was the erection on the outskirts of two textile mills, of which one still survives. They were the direct legacy of the domestic weaving industry of the eighteenth century, and lasted well into the twentieth, before changing economic circumstances led to the village's becoming largely a dormitory settlement for the surrounding towns, particularly Blackburn and Preston. Some, at least, of the attraction which drew, and draws, this kind of resident results from the peculiar fact that, although a river-side settlement, Ribchester has no bridge. The main street of the village, Church Street, might be expected to continue straight across the Ribble on a bridge, and had it done so Ribchester would be a rather different place from what it is. The apparent disadvantage of not having a bridge at the end of Church Street is partly made up for by the fact that a 'Ribchester Bridge' exists! It is not, however, and never has been, in Ribchester. The same factors which result in the lack of a bridge across the Ribble between Ribchester and Preston (discussed in the course of our consideration of the Roman roads, p. 2) meant that the site of a bridge in the vicinity of Ribchester had to be chosen with care, and in fact that site is about a mile upstream. Here, or hereabouts, there was a bridge which was newish when Stukeley saw it in 1725; its successor which did not survive the Great Flood of 1771 even to the stage of being used; and today's bridge was built to replace it in 1775.

With this thumbnail sketch of the development of Ribchester either side of its incorporation in the plans of a great expanding empire we leave the story of one Lancashire village. It is a village to which the author of this book, like thousands before him, have travelled, and doubtless thousands after him will follow, solely as a result of the fact that an army officer some nineteen hundred or more years ago decided that the site was an appropriate one for the siting of a fort. The picture has changed constantly throughout that period and will continue to do so. As I write, the Museum has embarked on ambitious plans to expand, with the aid of funds from the National Lottery. We can predict the Museum's development with reasonable certainty; we cannot predict what factors will operate to change life in the village or what new archaeological discoveries will take place to alter our ideas of life there in Roman times. We can say with absolute certainty that such changes will take place, and they will form the material for other books which other people will write.

A walk round the village

Starting from the Car Park, which lies to the north of the church, this route covers all the village's streets, and ends with a possible extra excursion to the outlying chapel at Stydd. Distance without the Stydd visit – about 1¼ miles (2 km). The Stydd visit would add about the same distance again, thereby trebling the total.

Leave the Car Park in a westerly direction (i.e. opposite to that from which it is approached by car). The road turns to the left and then right again. At this corner, on the left, is a kissing gate which gives access to a path outside the west wall of the churchyard. To your right is a depression in the field which marks the line of the south-western defences of the Roman fort. Another kissing gate leads into the churchyard.

The church evidently had a Norman predecessor (witness the decorated stones low in the south wall) and probably an earlier one (evidenced by the dedication to St Wilfrid and two fragments of late pre-Conquest crosses). It is now a thirteenth century building with additions. The east end of the chancel, with its external flat pilaster buttresses, has retained its group of three stepped lancet windows (unlike Whalley, where a large east window has replaced them). The south doorway of the chancel is of the same date, and the door itself retains a good bronze human head doubtless originally holding a (? sanctuary) knocker ring. The north (Dutton) chapel is in the Decorated style of the fourteenth century, while the piers of the south aisle, the south doorway, west tower and most of the remaining windows are Perpendicular. There is a west gallery, on Tuscan columns, of 1736 and dormer nave windows of the seventeenth century. The pulpit is of the seventeenth century, and elaborately carved. In the south-east corner of the churchyard, against the wall, is a raised Roman column base, and the sundial marks the point at which an excavation of 1833 located the steps of the *principia* strongroom.

Leave the churchyard by the east gate. To the right is *Churchgates*, created by Miss Greenall in 1906–7 (See Chapter 4). The stone block against the wall is one originally flanking the entrance from the courtyard to the cross-hall of the *principia*, but raised. To the left are the *Parish Hall* and *Museum* of 1914. Behind them, the eastern ends of the two *granaries* are exposed to view.

Proceeding along the river bank, you will see the *Rectory* of 1883 on the left. Where the road begins to bend left away from the river is roughly where the north-east wall of the Roman fort lay, and its line crossed where the river now runs, the south corner having been approximately on the present far bank of the river.

The visitor is now in *Church Street*, behind the first house of which, on the left hand side, the Helmet and its associated finds were discovered in 1796. The street is lined with eighteenth and nineteenth century cottages, of which some, particularly where the road widens in front of the White Bull Inn, show attractive date stones and the characteristic second-floor windows of handloom weaving.

The *White Bull Inn* itself has a date stone of 1707, but must be earlier. The columns which flank its entrance are said to be Roman, and may indeed be so, though this cannot be proved. The carved wooden *sign* dates from early in this century.

Continuing up Church Street, the visitor passes on the left *two eighteenth century brick houses*, one at right angles to the street and the other parallel to it. The latter has good dated cistern heads (1745). On the right, a little further on, a *lintel* is dated *1680* and has four hearts on it.

Turn right at the T-junction (Black Bull Inn on right) and follow *Blackburn Road* (a natural by-pass which, together with the lack of a bridge, has done much to preserve the character of the village) to the cross-roads. *Turn right on Water Street*. The extent of the Roman *vicus* is indicated by the discovery of Roman material outside the Black Bull and at the Blackburn Road/Water Street crossroads. 150 yards down Water Street, turn left into *Greenside*. The entrance to the remains of the *Roman Bath-house* is on the right.

From the Bath-house, the visitor may take the footpath which brings him out onto the river bank, then past the School, at the bottom of Church Street. Alternatively, he may return to Greenside, turn left, and retrace his steps to Water Street. Straight across is a passage which comes out at the entrance to the Car Park.

Stronger folk may *turn right* on Greenside, come out on Blackburn Road, turn right there, cross the bridge over the Duddel Brook (between the Ribchester Arms and the Stonebridge Restaurant). Then *turn left* into Stydd Lane to view the *Shireburn Almshouses* of 1728 and *St Saviour's Chapel*, the only remaining fragment of the medieval hospital once owned by the Knights Hospitallers. The chapel is a single-celled Norman building (see blocked door and two windows on the north side) with an Early English south doorway, later thirteenth century east and west windows, Perpendicular font and two windows, and seventeenth century pulpit and screen. It also has a double grave-slab of Sir Robert de Clitheroe and his wife, possibly the founders of the hospital, and another showing the sun and the moon in its corners. It has, however, no electricity and no pews, and evokes what many a small village church must have been like before later enlargements and restorations.

APPENDIX B

Inscriptions

Ribchester has yielded a good crop of Roman inscriptions, and a fairly high proportion of them are still in existence, largely thanks to the efforts of the Rev. Thomas Dunham Whitaker, who collected as many of them as possible and bequeathed them to his college, St John's, Cambridge. Those stones are now displayed in the Museum by the courtesy of the Master and Fellows of the College. Others from other sources have joined them. The following notes add to or correct the entries in RIB (Collingwood and Wright 1965). Some of the information below is included in the addenda and corrigenda in the second edition of RIB (1996). For further consideration of Camden and the Ribchester inscriptions, see Edwards 1998b. The RIB numbers are used here as the basis of the list.

RIB 583. Now in the Museum. The text, particularly from line 11 onwards, is badly worn, and the reconstruction here offered is a combination of that of RIB for lines 1–11 together with that suggested by Geza Alfoldy for lines 7–16.

DEO SAN(cto)/ [A]POLLINI MAPON(o)/ [PR]O SALVTE D(omini) N(ostri)/ [ET] N(vmeri) EQ(vitvm) SAR/ [M](atarvm) BREMETENN(acensivm)/ [G]ORDIANI/ IVL(ivs) ANTONI/ NVS C(entvrio) LEG-(ionis) VI/ VIC(tricis) DOMO/ MELITENIS/ [P]RAEP(ositvs) ET PRAEF(ectvs)/ V(otvm) S(olvit) L(ibens) L(aetvs) M(erito)/ [DE]DIC(atvm) PR(idie) KAL(endas) SEP(tembres)/ IMP(eratori) D(omino) N(ostro) GORDI/ [ANO A]VG(vsto) II ET PON/ PEIA[NO] CO(n)S(vlibvs).

To the holy god Apollo Maponus, for the welfare of our Lord [the Emperor] and of

Gordian's Own Unit of Sarmatian Cavalry of Bremetennacum, Julius Antoninus, centurion of the Sixth Victorious Legion, from Melitene, Commander and Prefect, willingly, freely and deservedly fulfils his vow. Dedicated on the first day of the Kalends of September in the year when Gordian Augustus was consul for the second time together with Pompeianus

The editors of RIB considered that the centurion's title was that of a *centurio regionarius,* and so it may have been. The year of dedication, if correctly discerned, would be A.D. 241 when Gordian III was Emperor. Melitene, the centurion's home, is modern Malataya, in eastern Anatolia, Turkey. The equation of Apollo with the Celtic god Mabon and the type of monument of which this stone formed the base are considered on p. 75.

RIB 584. Not, as RIB states, the stone seen by Camden 'in the house of T. Rodes'; this was RIB 586. See note on RIB 595, below, for Rhodes. Of this stone (RIB 584) Camden said 'Another little altar I saw there [i.e. Ribchester], cast out among rubbish stone'.

RIB 585. Kettlehurst Wood, Salesbury, the findspot of this stone, has not been located. Kettlehurst was named *c.* A.D. 1240 (Farrer and Brownbill 1906–1912, VI, 253, n. 7, citing Towneley MS HH 178) and the boundaries given there include the *Bruchet Gate* (? road through brushwood) which may be the Roman road, as far as Dinckley town field, and 'down by Mereclough to Ribble'. Mereclough is presumably, from its name, the boundary stream separating Salesbury and Dinckley. The name Kettlehurst was still in

Figure 49. Damaged dedication to the Mother Goddesses found in the course of the demolition of a cottage wall, 1980. The most recently discoved inscription from the site.

existence as late as 1730 for a holding of 12 acres (LRO DP 99) at which time it was described as lying in Salesbury and Dinckley, and was therefore, presumably astride the boundary of the two townships; it does not appear in a sale of most of the township of Salesbury in 1912 (LRO DDX 1271/1) or on Ordnance Survey maps. Camden's informant 'Mr Talbott', presumably 'Limping Thomas Talbot', second son of John Talbot of Salesbury (1501–1551), clerk of the Queen's records in the Tower of London before 1580, founder member of the Elizabethan Society of Antiquaries and in its membership list of 1590 and 'indefatigable in his researches into the records in his charge' (DNB) wrote that it 'standeth now att Saleburye under the stayres of the Grayner' (=granary).

RIB 586. This altar is the sole record on which the siting of an Asturian *ala* in garrison at Ribchester is based. In fact, the reading is less than certain and the numeration of the *ala* almost pure speculation. There is indeed no hint of any numeral in Camden (who, after all, saw the stone). The 'II' was allegedy read by T. W. Dilworth in 1824 (Anon. 1888). He, however, makes no mention of 'DEC' in line 4, so his evidence is suspect. 'II' probably became firmly included in the reading of this stone as a result of Haverfield's conjecture. It was this stone which Camden specifically said he saw on his second visit to Ribchester in 1603 'in the house of Thomas Rhodes'.

RIB 587. Now in the Museum. Experimental drawing restoration showed that line 4 probably ended PRO PRAE(tore) rather than PR(o) PR(aetore). This, which does not, of course, affect the sense in any way, is what was physically restored when the inscription was remounted in the 1970s. The suggestion came from R. P. Wright. For discussion of the significance of the inscription see Richmond 1945. The Museum also possesses a stone, recovered from the garden of the de Tabley Arms, Clayton-le-Dale, in 1988. It bears the following inscription: 'This stone taken/ out of ye Foundation/ of a *ROMAN* TEMPLE/ at RIBCHESTER/ By A: Cottam 1811'. This clearly refers to RIB 587, and also demonstrates the involvement of Adam Cottam (1755–1838) with Ribchester. He was a surveyor by occupation and lived at Whalley in what is known as the Pig House, which derives its name from the incorporation into one of its gables of a medieval animal carving, probably from Whalley Abbey. Cottam became wealthy enough to purchase for Whalley church a painting by Northcote and the organ discarded by Lancaster Parish Church, and to pay for the stone gateways at both ends of the churchyard. In his will he endowed almshouses at Whalley still to be seen in Mitton Road. He is said to have 'raised from obscurity as his pupil' the future Sir John Barrow (1764–1848) Secretary of the Admiralty. Barrow was born at Dragley Beck, Ulverston, attended Town End Grammar School there, and his monument, in the form of a lighthouse, stands on Hoad Hill above the town. The *Dictionary of National Biography* says that Barrow was taught mathematics by 'a sort of perambulating preceptor'. The probable connection between Cottam and Barrow is the Bradyll family. They owned both the Portfield estate at Whalley and Conishead Priory, two miles from Ulverston. In the second half of the eighteenth century the steward of the Bradyll family was Richard Cottam, who is likely to have been the father of Adam, though it has not proved possible to trace the family in detail. A painting of Adam Cottam hangs in the vestry of Whalley church. Cottam's connection with T. D. Whitaker is shown by the fact that he was the executor of Whitaker's will; his own will was witnessed by the Rev. Robert Whitaker, son of T. D. Whitaker.

RIB 589. A new reading and interpretation of this inscription have recently been offered (Speidel 1987) suggesting: IMP(eratori) CA[ES(ari) M(arco) AV]REL(io) A[NT(onino) AVG(vsto) ET]/ IMP(eratori) CA[ES(ari) L(vcio) AV]REL(io) VE[RO AVG(vsto)]/ VEX(illatio) EQ(vitatvm) [PROVINC]IAE [GERMANIAE]/ SVP(erioris) SE[X(to) CALPV]RN(io) [AGRICOLA CO(n)S(vlare)]

'*For the Emperor Caesar Marcus Aurelius Antoninus Augustus and for the Emperor Caesar Lucius Aurelius Verus Augustus a detachment of cavalrymen from the province of Upper Germany under Sextus Calpurnius Agricola, the emperors' praetorian legate [set this up]*'.

This reading requires minimal change in the letters of what appears to be a careful record. The stages of Speidel's reasoning on the implications of this reading are as follows:
– One or both of the two Germanies is/are the most likely source of such a vexillation; the Imperial dating to the joint reign of M. Aurelius and L. Verus gives the dates A.D. 161–169, Calpurnius Agricola being known to be Governor of Britain in 163; he was sent to Britain specifically to deal with an imminent war and is unlikely to have come alone, without bringing reinforcements; such a war or threat in the Pennines may well be the reason for the second abandonment of the Antonine Wall in 163.

As a consequence of this reading and interpretation of RIB 589, Speidel goes on to suggest that the inscription of the vexillation of the three British legions under Julius Verus at Newcastle upon Tyne (RIB 1322) means what it says, namely that they were sent *to* the Germanies, but that the occasion of the inscription was their return to Britain, presumably because they were required there. He further suggests that the absence of a substantial part of the legions may have been the occasion for a Brigantian revolt in A.D. 155, leading to the first abandonment of the Antonine Wall, and that the vexillations, on their return, remained together while assisting in the restoration of the Antonine Wall after its first abandonment.

Camden's correspondent, Thomas Braithwaite, gives the following interesting, if depressing, information on how this stone became defaced: 'Being a longe stone well hewed it haithe till nowe of laite laide over a fier in a kylne so that by reason of extreame heate the stone is broken in the middest and all of the lettres in the midest theirof are burned of saving the lettres at the beginninge of everie rowe ...'

RIB 590. Professor A. R. Birley has suggested the following for lines 7–9:
ET SEN(atvs) ET PAT(riae) MAR(ci)
ANTO(ni)/ GORDIAN(i) SE(m)PR/
[ONIAN(i) ROMAN(i) ... giving the names of the future Emperor Gordian I, when Governor in Britain, A.D. 216–219.

RIB 591. Stephens (1987) has proposed the following reading:
[IMP(peratori) CAES(ari) L(vcio) SEP-
TIM(io) SEVERO PIO]/ AVG(vsti) [ET
IMP(eratori) CAES(ARI) M(arco)
AVREL(io) ANTON(ino)]/ AVG(vsti) [ET
P(vblio) SEPTIMIO GETAE NOB(ilissimo)]/
CA[ES(ari) VEX(illatio) EQ(vitatvm) GER-
MANIAE SVPE]/ RIO[RIS L(vcio) ALF(eno)
SENECIONE LEG(atvs)] AV[G(vstorvm)
PR(o) PR(aetore) ...]

For the Emperor Caesar Lucius Septimius Pius Augustus and the Emperor Caesar Marcus Aurelius Antoninus Augustus and Publius Septimius Geta most noble Caesar a detachment of cavalry from Upper Germany under Lucius Alfenus Senecio, the Emperors' praetorian legate [set this up].

The province in lines 4–5 could equally well be INFERIOR, and the Governor's name depends upon the best fit to line length and the fact that Alfenus Senecio has left more inscriptions than Valerius Pudens. EQ(vitvm) is preferred to PR(ovinciae) or EX(ercitvs) in line 4 on the basis that Rib-

chester is a known cavalry fort. Stephens thinks that fighting rather than building was the most likely function of a vexillation, and that the Imperial expedition of A.D. 208 is the most likely context. He suggests that the vexillation recorded at Manchester on RIB 576 has the same background and points to a number of other British inscriptions with continental affinities and an inscription from Africa Proconsularis recording an *expeditio Britannicae.* He explains the presence of vexillations at or near known forts by the greater ease of keeping them supplied, paid and amused there, while awaiting deployment in the expedition.

RIB 592. Now in the Museum. It was recorded at Browsholme Hall in Anon. 1815. Pennant, in 1773, saw it 'fixed in the wall of a small house near the church' (Pennant 1801, 93).

RIB 593. Now in the Musuem.

RIB 594. The beginning of the RIB entry reads 'Tombstone with origin unspecified recorded for Camden, who from the mention of *ala Sarmatarum* assigned it to Ribchester'. In fact, in the earliest edition of *Britannia* in which an account of this inscription appears (1607), Camden says 'Ala Sarmatarum hoc in loco egisse et illa superiori inscriptione [RIB 595] et hac, quae antea plures annos iuxta reperta, videatur'. This is translated by Philemon Holland thus: 'That, ALA SARMATARVM, that is, a wing of Sarmatian horsemen abode in this place, it may seeme, as well by that former inscription, as by this, that many yeeres before was found hard by'. This is fairly unequivocal; the RIB statement of unspecified origin probably derives from Hübner's quotation (CIL VII 229) from Gruter (1560–1627), *Inscriptiones antiquae totius orbis Romani* (Heidelberg, 1603) 'incerto loca effossa in Anglia missaque ad D. Giulielmus Camdenum'. One can only presume that Camden, by 1607, had more precise information about the findspot than

Gruter; he may well have got it on his 1603 visit to Ribchester.

Camden's source for the inscription is given as 'Out of William Lambards notes'. William Lambard(e) (1536–1601) was the historian of Kent and author of several legal books, who turned over his notes for an intended history of Britain when he learnt of the latter's projected *Britannia.* Whitaker (1872–6, I, 28) suggested that Lambarde may have got his information from his friend, Laurence Nowell. The latter (? –1576) Dean of Lichfield and brother of Alexander Nowell, Dean of St Paul's, had Lambarde as his pupil in the London chambers of Nowell's younger brother, Robert, Attorney General of the Court of Wards. Laurence left a MS Vocabularium Saxonicum which passed to Lambarde. The Nowell family came from Read in Lancashire, seven miles east of Ribchester, and in view of Camden's Lancashire connections (see note on RIB 595 below) his acquisition of information by that means is perfectly feasible.

RIB 595. The sketch reproduced in RIB shows a tombstone similar to that found in the river bank in 1876 (see p. 49 and fig. 23) but with the horseman riding to the spectator's left. Although this is something of a rarity, there is no reason to doubt the accuracy of this element of the sketch. Other details of the scene are described in the accompanying letter with great precision. Schleiermacher (1984) lists a total of 134 tombstones of this type from the Empire (incidentally not including either this or the 1876 stone). In ten cases it is not possible to be sure about the direction of the figure's movement. Of the remaining 124, only 8 travel to the left. A stone such as Schleiermacher's No. 56 (from Cherchel, Algeria) supports the contention that leftward travel makes the depiction of the spearing of a foe much more awkward. On this stone, Dazas, from Coh. VI Delmatarum, holds his lozenge-shaped shield nearly horizontal across his body, enabling us to see his

shoulders and the hem of his tunic, while his right arm has been brought round to hold his spear vertically along the neck and forequarters of his horse on its left side.

Camden's informant on this stone, as on RIB 589, was Thomas Braithwaite of Beaumont near Lancaster, a relative by marriage. Braithwaite's wife was Camden's cousin, their respective mothers being sisters, *nées* Curwen, from Poulton Hall in what is now Morecambe. Braithwaite tells Camden, in his letter (transcribed in Edwards 1997) that he has been to Ribchester specially 'in Crissinmass laste' to see the stone, taking with him Mr John Dewhurst of Dewhurst as witness to his accuracy. Unfortunately, they did not even have a stab at reading the letters lower on the stone, represented in the sketch by five lines of dashes. Thomas Rhodes, mentioned under RIB 586, was evidently the local 'archaeological correspondent' at the time, as Braithwaite's reason for visiting Ribchester was to see the stone 'which goodman Roades and others did report of'.

RIB 598. This was found, despite RIB, in the 'west' gate of the fort in 1899 (Garstang 1899). This is surely part of milestone bearing part of the names of the Emperor Trajan Decius (A.D. 249–251) as do RIB 2268, also from Ribchester, and RIB 2271, from near Lancaster.

RIB 599. Included by RIB under Ribchester, this stone is built into the fabric of Whalley church. Within this church is a Roman altar and outside it a possible Roman building stone. They may have been brought from Ribchester, or there may be a nearer site from which they came. The imprecisely identified findspot of RIB 585 may be evidence of the carriage of Roman stones from Ribchester towards Whalley, ending in that case in its falling from the cart and not being recovered. Alternatively, the stone may be evidence of a rural temple.

Addition

Altar found in the autumn of 1982 in the course of the demolition of a cottage in Church Street. It reads:

MATRIBVS/ MARV[L]L[A]/ INSEQVE/ NTIS V(otvm) S(olvit)/ L(ibens) L(aetvs) M(erito).

To the Mother Goddesses Marulla (?wife/daughter) of Insequens willingly and freely discharged her vow.

The omission of the relationship of Marulla, a feminine name, to Inseqens is not uncommon 'in barbarous parts of the Empire'. There are several points of interest about this dedication, particularly that RIB 586 from Ribchester is also a dedication to the Mothers, and that in the church of Lund (Newton-with-Clifton) in the Fylde, some 15 miles west of Ribchester, the font is a Roman altar bearing sculptures of the mothers and dancing figures, though it is uninscribed. Over 60% of instances of the name Insequens occur in Noricum (modern Austria).

Inscriptions on other materials (Instrumentum domesticum)

Recorded in RIB II (Published in eight fascicules, 1990–1995) are the following from Ribchester:

2415.31 (Stamp on handle of camp kettle found with the Helmet in 1796); 2423.7 (*Graffiti* on the helmet); 2425.6 (The AVE MEA VITA ring); 2491.62 and 2491.143 (*Graffiti* on tiles); The remainder are all *graffiti* on pottery of various types. 2494.87: 2494.210: 2497.26: 2501.158: 2501.330: 2501.362: 2501.553: 2501.582: 2501.632: 2501.668: 2501.783: 2501.854: 2501.864: 2503.87: 2503.88: 2503.352: 2503.466: 2503.547.

Bibliography

There follow two lists of references. The first includes publications referred to in the text which are not directly related to the Roman fort at Ribchester, together with the 'standard' study of the province (Frere 1987) and one or two regional studies. The second list is a near-complete bibliography for the Roman fort; it includes all substantial references for the site together with a number of minor ones. It does not, of course, include passing references in general works on Roman Britain or on aspects of Roman history and archaeology. (Numbers in brackets are the relevant pages for Ribchester; dates in square brackets are the actual dates of publication of journals, as opposed to the year for which they were issued)

Edwards, B. J. N., 1966 'Roman Lancashire', 95–104 in Jarrett, M. G. and Dobson, B (eds).

Ekwall, E., 1922 *The Place Names of Lancashire* (Chetham Soc. vol. 81), Manchester.

Farrer, W. and Brownbill, J. (1906–12) *The Victoria History of the County of Lancaster*, 8 vols.

Frere, S. S., 1987 (3rd. edn.) *Britannia*.

Jarrett, M. G. and Dobson, B. (eds), 1966 *Britain and Rome*, Kendal

Jones, G. D. B., 1968 'The Romans in the North-West', *Northern History* 3 (1968) 1–26.

——, 1970a 'Roman Lancashire', *Arch. Jnl.* 126 (1970) 11–19.

Margary, I. D., 1967 (Rev. edn.) *Roman Roads in Britain*.

Randall, H. J., 1933 '*Splendide Mendax*', *Antiquity* 7 (1933) 49–60.

Rivet, A. L. F. and Smith, C. (1979) *The Placanames of Roman Britain*.

Robinson, H. R., 1975 *The Armour of Imperial Rome*.

Schleiermacher, M., 1984 *Römische Reitergrabsteine. Die kaiserzeitliche Reliefs des triumphierenden*, Bonn.

Shotter, D.C. A., 1973 *Roman Lancashire*, Clapham.

——, 1993 *Romans and Britons in North West England*, Lancaster

Anonymous items, by date

1815 *Description of Browsholme Hall ... and of the parish of Waddington.* (p. 13 & pl.)

1841 'Gold Coin of Trajan', *Num. Chron.* 3 (1841) 60.

1851a HSLC 3 (1851) 26.

1851b HSLC 3 (1851) 105.

1851c HSLC 3 (1851) 113.

1888 'The Roman Altar in the Bowling Green', *Stonyhurst Mag.*, No. 37, 139–140.

1891 LCAS 8 (1890) [1891] 161–166.

1893 LCAS 10 (1892) [1893] 135.

1901 'Excursion to Ribchester', *Trans. Burnley Lit. & Sci. Club* 17 (1899) 83–85.

1914 'Roman Road Between Ribchester and Overborough', *Lancs. Nat.* 6 (1914), No. 70 (N.S. No. 68), 370.

1927 'Excavations at Ribchester', *Ant. Jnl.* 7 (1927) 323.

1970 *Britannia* I (1970) 281, 311.

1971 *Ibid.*, II (1971) 255.

1973 *Ibid.*, IV (1973) 283.

1975 *Ibid.*, VI (1975) 239.

1977 *Ibid.*, VIII (1977) 385.

1978 *Ibid.*, IX (1978) 429.

1979 *Ibid.*, X (1979) 291.

1981 *Ibid.*, XII (1981) 331.

1990 *Ibid.*, XXI (1990) 328.

1992 *Ibid.*, XXIII (1992) 276–279.

1994 *Ibid.*, XXV (1994) 298.

——, *The Roman Fort at Ribchester*, National Trust.

Newspapers: a few significant items, in date order

Blackburn Mail, 3 August, 1796 [Discovery of the Helmet, etc.]

Preston Pilot, 11 February, 1837 [Discovery of the Bath-house]

Blackburn Standard, 1898 [Series on The Roman Military Station at Ribchester]

Manchester Guardian , 4 May, 1908 [Description of Thomas May's excavations]

Manchester Guardian, 11 September, 1915 [Opening of the Museum]

Preston Herald, 11 September, 1915 [Opening of the Museum]

Warrington Examiner, 7 November, 1931 [Death of Thomas May]

Abram, W. A., 1876 'Account of a Roman Sculptured Stone Slab found at Ribchester', HSLC 28 (1876) 190–193 & f'piece.

——, 1877 *A History of Blackburn, Town and Parish.* (11–20).

——, 1878 PSAL₂ 7 (1876–78), 30–34.

Andrew, W. J., (1905) 'Buried Treasure: some traditions records and facts', BNJ 1 (1903–4), [1905]9–59 (11–15).

——, (1908) 'Buried Treasure: some traditions records and facts', JBAA2 9 (1908), 8–15 (10–12).

Baines, E., (1801) *The History of the County Palatine and Duchy of Lancaster.* (III, 376–390).

——, (1836) *Ibid.*, 2nd edn (376–382).

——, (1868–1870) *Ibid.*, 3rd edn, J. Harland, 2 vols. (II, 104–107).

——, (1888–1893) *Ibid.*, 4th edn, J. Croston, 5 vols. (II, 91–98).

Bell, W. (1852) 'On the Bronze Mask attached to the Roman Helmet found at Ribchester', *Gent's Mag.*, N.S. 38 (1852) 450–453.

Brailsford, J. W., (1951) *Guide to the Antiquities of Roman Britain* (British Museum) (67 & plXXV, 4) (and other editions).

Bruce, J. C., (1855) 'On the Roman Antiquities from the North of England in the Libraries of Trinity and St John's Colleges, Cambridge', *Arch. Jnl.* 12 (1855) 213–228 (225–228).

Buxton, K. and Howard-Davies, C. (forthcoming) *Brigantia to Britannia: Excavations on the site of the Roman Fort at Ribchester, 1980 and 1989/90.*

Camden, W., (1586) *Britannia, sive florentissimum regnorum, Angliae, Scotiae, Hiberniae, et insularum jacentium ex intima antiquitate chorographica descriptio.* (432)

——, (1587) *Ibid.*, 2nd edn (510–511).

——, (1590) *Ibid.*, 3rd edn (617).

——, (1594) *Ibid.*, 4th edn (583).

——, (1600) *Ibid.*, 5th edn (680).

——, (1607) *Ibid.*, 6th edn (613–616).

——, (1610) *Ibid.*, 7th edn, tr. Holland, P. (750–752) (Rep. 1637).

——, (1695) *Britain*, ed. Gibson, E., (cols 791–793).

——, (1722) *Ibid.*, 2 vols. (cols. 972–974)

——, (1789) *Britannia*, ed. Gough, R., 3 vols. (III, 129–130 and 138–139).

——, (1809) *Ibid.*, 4 vols., (377–378).

Collingwood, R. G. and Wright, R. P., (1965) *The Roman Inscriptions of Britain, vol. I, Inscriptions on Stone.* (194–210 (items 583–599) and 710 (items 2268–2269).

Conway, R. S. and Hopkinson, J. H., (1908) [Letter to the *Manchester Guardian*, quoted (not quite in its entirety)], *Antiquary* 44 (1908), 201–202.

Corry, J., (1825) *History of Lancashire* (277–286).

Crosby, A. (ed.)(1998) *Leading the Way*, Preston.

Cuming, H. S., (1869) 'On Ancient Sieves and Colanders', JBAA 25 (1869) 244–250 (246).

Eames, J. V. H., (1956) [Exploratory work at Ribchester], JRS 46 (1956), 125.

Edwards, B. J. N., (1972) *Ribchester, Lancashire* (The National Trust).

——, (1992) *The Ribchester Hoard*, Preston.

——, (1994) 'How did Thomas Pennant cross the Ribble?', *Lancs. Local Hist.*, 9 (1994) 8–11.

——, (1997) 'The Ribchester 'Gold' Brooch', *Lancs. Local Hist.*, 12 (1997) 1–10.

——, (1998a) 'The Romans and Before', 1–28 in Crosby, A. (ed.)1998.

——, (1998b) *William Camden, his Britannia and Some Roman Inscriptions*, Lecture delivered at the Senhouse Roman Museum, Maryport, 27 October, 1998, Maryport.

—— and Webster, P. V. (eds) (1985) *Ribchester Excavations, Pt. 1, Excavations within the Roman Fort*, Cardiff.

——, (1987) *Ibid., Pt. 2, Excavations in the Civil Settlement, A. The Structures*, Cardiff.

——, (1988) *Ibid., Pt. 3, Ibid., B. Pottery and Coins*, Cardiff.

——, (forthcoming) *Ibid., Pt. 4, Finds from Roman Ribchester.*

Frere, S. S. and Tomlin, R. S. O.,(eds) (1990–1995) *The Roman Inscriptions of Britain*, volume II, *Instrumentum domesticum.* Published in eight fascicules, with M. Roxan as an additional editor for fascicule I, Gloucester.

Garstang, J., [1898] *Roman Ribchester: being the Report of the Excavations made on the site during 1898* (Ribchester Excavation Fund Report, 1898), Preston, London and Oxford.

——, [1899a] *Ribchester Excavation Fund 1899: Interim Report on the Excavations resumed during 1899 upon the site of Roman Ribchester.*

——, (1899b) 'Roman Ribchester', *Antiquary* 35 (1899) 80–84.

——, (1900) 'The Ribchester Excavations, 1899', *Antiquary* 36 (1900) 184–186.

——, (1901) 'Roman Ribchester', *Trans. Burnley Lit. and Sci. Club* 17 (1899) [1901], 11–13.

——, (1902a) 'List of Roman Remains from Ribchester', HSLC 53 (1901) [1902], 189–208.

——, (1902b) 'The Ribchester Temple', HSLC 53 (1901) [1902], 208–216.

Harrison, W., (1914) 'The Roman Road between Ribchester and Overborough', LCAS 31 (1913) [1914], 69–87.

Haverfield, F. J., (1893) 'Romano-British Inscriptions 1892–1893', *Arch. Jnl.* 50 (1893), 279–307 (286).

——, (1903) 'The Ribchester "temple"', HSLC 53 (1902) [1903]197–202.

——, (1915) *Roman Britain in 1914* (Brit. Acad. Supp. Pap.,III) (12–13, 45–46).

Heathcote, W. H., 1889 'Ribchester', LCAS 7 (1889) [1890] 229–235.

Hildyard, E. J. W., (1954) 'A Triple-headed Bucket Mount', *Ant. Jnl.* 34 (1954) 225–229.

Hinde, J. H., (1846) 'Bremetenracum: on the site of Bremetenracum in the Notitia and Bremetonacum in the Itinerary, and on the bearing of this question on Horsley's theory of Secondary Stations 'per lineam valli', with some speculations on the sites of certain other Stations in the Notitia and Itinerary', *Arch. Ael.* ₁ 4 (1846) 109–118.

——, (1851) 'Bremetenracum of the *Notitia*', *Gent's Mag.* 139 (1851) 640–642.

Hopkinson, J. H., (1911) *The Roman Fort at Ribchester*, Manchester.

——, (1916) *Ibid.*, 2nd edn, London and Manchester.

——, (1928) *Ibid.*, 3rd edn, Rev. and Enlarged D. Atkinson, Manchester.

Horsley, J., (1732) *Britannia Romana: or the Roman Antiquities of Britain.* (Rep., Newcastle upon Tyne, 1974) (Bk. I, 302–303)

Hübner, E. (ed.), (1873) *Corpus Inscriptionum Latinarum*, Vol. 7. (58–61 (Nos. 218–230, s. v. *Coccium*)

Jackson, R. P. J. and Craddock, P. T. (1995) 'The Ribchester Hoard: A Descriptive and Technical Study', 75–102 in Raftery, B (ed.) 1995.

Jones, G. D. B., 1970b 'Ribchester Roman Fort', *Arch. Jnl.* 126 (1970) 53–55.

Just, J., (1846) 'On the Roman Military Road between Manchester and Ribchester', *Trans. Manchester Lit. and Phil. Soc.* ₂ 7 (1846), 1–21.

——, (1849) 'On the Roman Roads in Lancashire, with a Particular Account of the Tenth Iter of Antoninus', HSLC 1 (1849), 68–76.

Just, J. and Harland, J., (1851) 'On Roman Ribchester', JBAA 6 (1851), 229–251.

Leigh, C., (1700) *The Natural History of Lancashire, Cheshire, and the Peak, in Derbyshire …*, Oxford. (Bk. III, 1–10).

Leland, J. See Smith, L. Toulmin (ed.)

Morgan, T., (1872) 'On the Worship of Apollo in Britain', JBAA 28 (1872), 337–346 (343–346).

Pennant, T., (1801) *A Tour from Downing to Alston-Moor.* (92–99).

Pink, W. D. (ed.) (1885) *Lancashire and Cheshire Antiquarian Notes*, Leigh. (Vol. 1, Nos. 17 and 35).

Raftery, B. (ed.) (1995) *Sites and Sights of the Iron Age; Essays … presented to Ian Mathieson Stead.*

Richmond, I. A., (1945) 'The Sarmatae, *Bremetennacum Veteranorum* and the *Regio Bremetennacensis*', JRS 35 (1945), 15–29.

Ross, P., (1916a) 'Roman Roads in Yorkshire: Ribchester to York. The road between Downham Park and Bramham Moor', *Bradford Antiquary* N.S. VI, (1916), 33–64.

——, (1916b) 'The Roman Road from Ribchester to Low Borrow Bridge (near Tebay), through the Forest of Bolland, Lonsdale and Howgill Fells', *Bradford Antiquary* N.S. VI (1916), 243–266.

——, (1916c) 'The First Stage of the Roman Road from Ribchester to York', *Bradford Antiquary* N.S. VI (1916), 267–272.

Sidebotham, S., n.d. *Bremetennacum.*

Smith, L. Toulmin (ed.) (1921) *The Itinerary of John Leland*, 5 vols. (Vol. 2, 21).

Smith, T. C. and Shortt, J., (1890) *The History of the Parish of Ribchester in the County of Lancaster*, London and Preston. (1–41, 151–154).

Speidel, M. P., (1987) 'The Chattan War, the Brigantian Revolt and the Loss of the Antonine Wall', *Britannia* XVIII (1987) 233–237.

Stephens, G. R., (1987) 'A Severan Vexillation at Ribchester', *Britannia* XVIII (1987) 239–242.

Stukeley, W., (1776) *Iter Boreale* (2nd edn) (36–38).

Thompson, F. H., (1958) 'A Romano-British Pottery Kiln at North Hykeham, Lincolnshire: with an Appendix on the Typology, Dating and Distribution of 'Rustic' ware in Great Britain', *Ant. Jnl.* 38 (1958), 15–51 (42).

Townley, C., (1815) 'Account of Antiquities discovered at Ribchester, in a letter from Charles Townley, Esq., F.R.S. & F.S.A. to the Rev. John Brand, M.A., Secretary to the Society of Antiquaries', *Vetusta Monumenta* IV (1815) 1–12.

Toynbee, J. M. C., (1964) *Art in Britain under the Romans*, Oxford. (109, 153, 192, 202–203, 298).

——, (1962) *Art in Roman Britain.*

Walters, H. B., (1915) *Select Bronzes in the British Museum.* (Pl. LXXII and 2 pages of accompanying unnumbered text).

Watkin, W. T., (1878) 'Roman Ribchester', HSLC 30 (1878), 1–26.

——, (1883) *Roman Lancashire*, Liverpool. (125–163).

——, (1888) 'Recent Discoveries of Roman Remains in Britain', *Reliquary*, n. s. 2, (1888), 26–29 (27).

Weston, S., (1798) 'Observations on Mr Townley's Antique Bronze Helmet, found at Ribchester in Lancashire', *Arch.* 13 (1798), 223–226.

Whitaker, J., (1773) *The History of Manchester*, 2nd edn (176–187, 270).

Whitaker, T. D., (1801) *An History ... of the Ancient Parish of Whalley ...* (12–23).

——, (1806) *Ibid.*, 2nd edn

——, (1818) *Ibid.*, 3rd edn, (11–28).

——, (1823) *An History ... of Richmondshire in the North Riding of the County of York; ...* (458–462).

——, (1872–1876) *[Whalley].*, 4th edn, Nicholls, J. G. and Lyons, P. A. (I, 11–41).

Abbreviations

Ant. Jnl. – Antiquaries Journal.
Arch. Ael₁ – Archaeologia Aeliana (Newcastle upon Tyne), first series.
Arch. – Archaeologia.
Arch. Jnl. – Archaeological Journal.
BNJ *– British Numismatic Journal.*
Gent's Mag. – Gentleman's Magazine.
HSLC *– Transactions of the Historic Society of Lancashire and Cheshire* (Liverpool).
JBAA *– Journal of the British Archaeological Association.*
JRS *– Journal of Roman Studies.*

LCAS *– Transactions of the Lancashire and Cheshire Antiquarian Society* (Manchester).
Lancs. Local Hist. – Lancashire Local Historian.
Lancs. Nat. – Lancashire Naturalist.
Num. Chron. – Numismatic Chronicle.
PSAL₂ *– Proceedings of the Society of Antiquaries of London,* second series.
T. Burnley Lit. and Sci. Club– Transactions of the Burnley Literary and Scientific Club.
T. Manchester Lit. and Phil. Soc. – Transactions of the Manchester Literary and Philosophical Society.

Index

Note: the index does *not* cover the illustrations or appendices.

Occasional Papers from the Centre for North-West Regional Studies

The Buildings of Georgian Lancaster, (revised edition), 2000, Andrew White £6.95
A History of Linen in the North West, 1998, ed. Elizabeth Roberts £6.95
History of Catholicism in the Furness Peninsula, 1998, Anne C. Parkinson £6.95
Vikings in North West England – The Artifacts, 1998, B. J. N. Edwards £6.95
Sharpe, Paley and Austin, Lancaster Architectural Practice 1836–1942, 1998, James Price £6.95
Romans and Britons (revised edition), 1997, David Shotter £6.95
Victorian Terraced Housing in Lancaster, 1996, Andrew White and Michael Winstanley £6,95
Walking Roman Roads in the Fylde and the Ribble Valley, 1996, Philip Graystone £5.95
Romans in Lunesdale, 1995, David Shotter and Andrew White £6.50
Roman Route Across the Northern Lake District, Brougham to Moresby, 1994, Martin Allan £5.95
Walking Roman Roads – East Cumbria, 1994, Philip Graystone £5.95
S. Martin's College, 1993, Peter S. Gedge and Lois R. Louden £5.95
Lydia Becker and the Cause, 1992, Audrey Kelly £5.95
From Lancaster to the Lakes: the region in literature, 1992, ed. Keith Hanley and Alison Milbank £5.95
Walking Roman Roads in Bowland, 1992, Philip Graystone £5.50
Windermere in the 19th century, 1991, Ed. Oliver M. Westall £4.95
T. D. Smith's: A Traditional Grocer 1858–1981, 1991, Ed. Michael Winstanley £4.95
The Roman Fort and Town of Lancaster, 1990, David Shotter and Andrew White £4.95
Grand Fashionable Nights: Kendal Theatre, 1989, Margaret Eddershaw £3.95
Rural Life in SW Lancashire, 1988, Alistair Mutch £3.95
The Diary of Willian Fisher of Barrow, 1986, ed. Willian Rollinson & Brett Harrison £2.95
Popular Leisure and the Music Hall in 19th century Bolton, 1982, Robert Poole £2.95
Richard Marsden and the Preston Chartists, 1981, J. E. King £2.95

Each of these titles may be ordered by post from:

CNWRS
Fylde College
University of Lancaster
Bailrigg, Lancaster LA1 4YF

Fax: 01524 594725
email: christine.wilkinson@lancaster.ac.uk
www: http://www.lancs.ac.uk/users/cnwrs

Postage will be £1 per copy.
Please make cheques payable to 'The University of Lancaster'.
Titles are available from all good booksellers in the region.